THE KEY
TO
CAREER SUCCESS

THE KEY TO CAREER SUCCESS

Follow the Rules of Perception

Sanxing Sun

T. L. Tower Press

The Key to Career Success
Follow the Rules of Perception

Copyright©2007 by Sanxing Sun. All rights reserved. No part of this book may be reproduced in any form, except for brief quotations in a review, without the prior permission of the publisher. For more information, please visit: www.tltower.com.

International Standard Book Number:

ISBN-10   0-9785590-0-2

ISBN-13   978-0-9785590-0-7

Library of Congress Catalog Card Number:

LCCN   2007902082

Published by T. L. Tower

Printed in the United States of America

This Book Is Dedicated to You

PROPERTY OF:
Cowichan Career Resource Centre
#301 - 80 Station St., Duncan, B.C.
V9L 1M4   Phone: 748-9880

CONTENTS

ACKNOWLEDGMENTS	11
PREFACE	13
INTRODUCTION	15

PART I
THE PRINCIPLES

1 PERCEPTION MATTERS — 21

Perception Is Reality — 21

Perception Is a Force — 24

From Appearance to Perception — 27

2 THE FORMATION OF PERCEPTION — 29

Perception Forms Early — 29

Personality Matters — 37

The Three Essential Qualities — 38

Contents

The Negativity Effect	42
The Fundamental Attribution Error	43
Presentation Is Everything	45

PART II
IMPLEMENT THE PRINCIPLES

3 ACQUIRING DYNAMISM — 51
Be Confident	51
Be Committed	58
Take Action	63
Overcome Barriers	64

4 DELIVERING RESULTS — 69
Deliver Results Early and Consistently	69
Work on Achievable Tasks	70
Build on Strengths and Success	74
Focus on Priority	76
Result-Oriented Learning	78
Deliver Emotional Results	81
Deliver a Competent You	85

5 COMMUNICATION — 88
The Role of Communication	88
The Challenge of Communication	89
Be Committed to Your Message	91
Be Prepared with Your Message	96
Deliver a Great Presentation	99
Avoid Unnecessary Debate	104
Excel in Debate	109

Contents

Keep Your Cool	121
Be a Good Listener	124

6 RELATIONSHIP 126

Perception Creates Relationship	126
Treat Yourself Well First	127
Be Open and Direct	130
See Each Relationship in Advance	132
With Your Boss	133
With Your Reports	141
With Your Peers	148

7 THE ULTIMATE SECRETS 156

Don't Be Overly Concerned with Perception	156
Synchronize Your Heart and Mind	157
Lighten Up	161

PART III
REVIEW AND ADJUSTMENT

8 MAKING CHANGES 165

If You Are Unsatisfied	165
If You Are Already Happy	168

EPILOGUE	173
INDEX	175

ACKNOWLEDGMENTS

Many thanks to editors Pam Guerrier and Shellie Hurrle. Their editing and feedback have lifted the book to an even higher level.

PREFACE

Given the fact that there are already so many books on career development, you might ask why I would also write a book on the topic. The reason is that I have something new to offer. You will gain a new perspective on this matter after reading the book. I can guarantee that you haven't heard of some of the concepts anywhere else.

In this book, you may see certain things that are contrary to common belief. I didn't write them to entertain, but to share with readers what I think everyone must know. The goal is to make sure that readers can see something insightful, practical, and to the point, and they can truly learn something. I hope you will see that the book is a simple yet helpful tool.

INTRODUCTION

You probably already know that not all top students necessarily do well after leaving school. If you excelled in school, you might have experienced firsthand that what made you successful in the classroom loses much of its value at work. If you didn't quite make the honor roll, you certainly already know that it doesn't really matter. Perfect grades in school don't necessarily guarantee that you will have the same level of success afterward. It's not uncommon at all for an average student to outperform a top student in society.

Why doesn't doing well in school automatically mean you'll do well afterward? First, the way you are "graded" at work is determined differently. At school, your grades are determined by exams, which can measure your knowledge quite accurately. However, it's virtually impossible to use anything like an exam to measure your performance at work.

Instead, your performance at work is measured by others' opinions of you. No matter how good you really are, unless others recognize it and think you are good, you aren't good to others. It's always possible there is a big difference between how good you truly are and how good others' opinions of you are.

Second, there is a fundamental difference between your tasks at school and at work. Most school exams are designed to have correct answers. If you are a top student, you can be quite sure of your answers when taking exams. However, because most of the tasks at work will be new to you, the correct answers are often debatable. Rarely can you be 100 percent sure that you are doing the right thing, and that you'll achieve the expected results, even if you possess plenty of knowledge. As a result, if you have to be sure of everything in order to act confidently and decisively, you may find yourself feeling inadequate and uncomfortable at work.

Therefore, your knowledge won't automatically increase your value, unless you use the

Introduction

knowledge effectively and translate it into actions and results. There is no way that people can see exactly what is inside everyone else. If you don't appear to be good at what you do, it is almost a certainty that others won't think you are either.

This also means that it's important to know how people judge and form their opinions of one another. This will allow you to work more productively, and people will therefore be more likely to regard you highly. You need to know the rules in order to play the game.

The mind is an amazing thing. Although we may think we know how it works, it actually operates according to certain underlying principles that many people may not really know. Be sure that you attain the knowledge so that you can perform successfully in your career and be the best you can be in life.

PART I

THE PRINCIPLES

1

PERCEPTION MATTERS

PERCEPTION IS REALITY

Perception is reality. People's knowledge of everything is actually only their perception— what they think of it. No one can directly see the true nature of what they see. People first see something. Then they give it an explanation. And they will believe that their explanation of it—their perception— is what it is.

What does this have to do with you? It means that no matter how good you really are, you aren't good to others unless you can make them think you are. In other words:

It's not how good you are that matters. It's not how good you think you are that counts. It's how good other people perceive you that determines your reality.

Let's call it the law of perception. I want to use this rather strong statement to call your attention to others' perception of you.

How good you are matters, of course. It's just that no matter how good you are, and how strongly you believe it, in order for your talent to count, you have to make others regard you that way.

Of course, if you can be completely self-sufficient and live away from society, how others perceive you won't matter that much. But because most of us are members of society and have to rely on society's recognition to achieve success, we must pay attention to how others perceive us. If no one thinks you are valuable, it literally means that you aren't.

What's more, who you really are isn't necessarily who you are in society. Instead, you are always people's perception of you. Once other people's perception of you takes shape, whether accurate or not, it might as well be considered true and real. You can make the best use of

Perception Matters

this principle, but you can't change the way it works.

For example, let's say Mary and Mike are both running for city mayor. If more people perceive Mary to be better, Mary will likely win the election, regardless of who is actually more suitable for the position. Mike might actually be more qualified for the job, and it would thereby be better for the city if he were elected, but that's not how elections are decided. If you want to win an election, it is crucial to make voters perceive you as the better candidate.

This is also true in lawsuits. Facts don't necessarily determine each verdict. Instead, it's how the jury or the judge perceives the case that actually determines the verdict, even if it's about life and death.

We humans have known this truth for a long while, probably since the dawn of civilization. The origin of the word *person* is the Latin word *persona*, which means "a mask worn by a person, or a character played by an actor." Isn't the word *person* an amazingly accurate word?

George Berkeley, an Irish philosopher over two centuries ago, proclaimed the following: "To be is to be perceived." According to him, the quality of each person is only perceived and is only real to the perceiver, and what we know are only thoughts in our minds. Although his words might not make sense to everyone, there is actually a lot of truth to them.

Are there exceptions to the law of perception? It's obvious that school exams are exceptions, as are certain competitions such as track-and-field events. In such competitions, the outcome is determined by a standard measurement involving little subjective judgment. The law of perception doesn't apply to such situations because people's perceptions of each player play little or no role in determining the results.

PERCEPTION IS A FORCE

The power of perception lies in that it is not only reality, but also a strong, single-minded force that maintains the reality. The force is such that people want to see things consistent with their perceptions, and they tend to see these things only. People are unprepared to see, and therefore have difficulty seeing, those things that are incompatible with their perceptions.

Let's use two hypothetical people, Nancy and Henry, to illustrate the way it works. Due to the

Perception Matters

force of perception, if Nancy perceives Henry well, she'll be more likely to see the good that Henry does. As to any possible errors in Henry's work, she may not pay much attention to them, and she may not see them. Even if she does notice mistakes, she may not mention them, unless there is a problem that can't be ignored.

Likewise, if Nancy perceives Henry well, she will be more likely to understand him correctly and therefore agree with him. This is especially true in cases where people's understanding of the subject is still limited, for there will be plenty of room to either agree or disagree.

This is essentially what psychologists call the "halo effect." It refers to the fact that when we have good perceptions of others, it tends to make us see them as being entirely good, and we may only see their virtues as a result.

On the other hand, if Nancy perceives Henry less well, she will tend to behave differently, and she may even become quite unreasonable with him. Psychologists refer to this as the "horns effect."

There are differences among people on this matter. Some people can be rather objective, while others can be quite the opposite. The cause of the problem is the perceptions, thoughts, or beliefs in people's minds. It is the force of perception in action.

The ultimate power of the force is that it can change you and turn you into what really fits the perception, because the self-fulfilling prophecy may take effect eventually. According to self-fulfilling prophecy, others' perception of you can influence your behavior significantly. If you are surrounded by a certain perception of you for an extended period, you may live up to the perception in the end.

This is quite logical. When what you experience is mostly positive, your confidence level will be boosted, you'll be encouraged to do even better, and you'll be more likely to prove that you can. If you experience the opposite, it can affect you quite differently.

German humanist and philosopher Johann Wolfgang Goethe, one of the greatest human minds in history, said, "Treat a man as he can and should be, and he will become as he can and should be." Self-fulfilling prophecy bestows perception with magic power. Others' perception of you promotes such changes in you that you may eventually well fit the perception, even if it wasn't quite right initially.

Perception Matters 27

Therefore, how people perceive you matters critically to your career success. It not only determines your current reality at the workplace or in society, but also determines the experience you'll have with other people. It can have a huge impact on your future prospects.

FROM APPEARANCE TO PERCEPTION

About five hundred years ago, Italian statesperson and political philosopher Niccoló Machiavelli wrote, "The great majority of mankind is satisfied with appearances, as though they were realities." This statement reveals an important truth about perception.

How do people acquire their perceptions of others? They do it according to what can be easily seen. People will make assumptions when they form perceptions, and the assumptions are often based on appearances. This is often a subconscious process. It usually occurs without the perceiver's knowledge.

While the appearance can be easily seen, what is underneath may not be seen easily, even if it's the true nature. As a result, there is almost always a close association between perception and appearance. For example, if you cover gold with dirt, most people will likely think that it's all dirt.

Therefore, always keep in mind that appearances matter. Merely being good enough is not good enough. Don't assume that people will easily know you correctly. Do help them see the real you, and make it easy for them to realize that you are good enough.

In other words, be sure that you use your talents in the most effective, productive way possible. This way, you'll help others regard you as being good as you truly are. I am sure that you already have all the qualifications to be successful; otherwise, you wouldn't have picked up this book. But those qualifications alone don't necessarily ensure success. It's important to use your talents effectively in order to make them really count. If you want to do well in life, never forget this important matter.

That will be the main theme of the book. We will discuss how to perform effectively so that you will look your best, be your best, and be as successful as you deserve to be.

2

THE FORMATION OF PERCEPTION

PERCEPTION FORMS EARLY

Others don't need all the information about you to form their perception of you. They do it according to the information they receive early on. As a result, the initial image you present plays a dominant role in shaping people's perception of you. If you reveal the right information about yourself early enough, you'll help others form a desirable perception of you.

In a psychological study conducted by psychologist Edward Jones, two groups of people were asked to watch a student taking a quiz of thirty multiple-choice problems. Both groups saw the student got fifteen answers correct. However, for the first group, the student got most of the correct answers early on in the test. For the second group, the student got most of the correct answers later on in the test. When the two groups of people were asked to evaluate the student afterward, the first group gave the student a much better assessment than the second group did.

Numerous studies have shown the same results. When people make judgments of others, they usually weigh early information much more heavily than later information. What's more, people often resist making corrections to their initial impressions of others, even if there is plentiful evidence telling them that they should. Using early information to form perceptions of others is a psychological phenomenon called "primacy effect."

As this applies to the workplace, when you join a new organization, the early period is the critical window of time. It's important to demonstrate early on that you have a productive personality and the required competency for your position.

If you send out a lot of positive information about yourself in the beginning, others will

The Formation of Perception   31

almost certainly perceive you in a positive way. If you give off a lot of counterproductive information about yourself during this critical period, others are almost certainly going to perceive you differently. Others' perception of you can form very fast. It can take shape before you know it.

Therefore, wherever you go, be sure to act the way you want to be seen as early as possible. Others aren't prepared for a lengthy, systematic study of you. They won't wait patiently for you to say, "Okay, I'm ready. You can judge me now." If you don't provide others with correct information about you early on, you'll allow them to misinterpret you.

You might wonder why we humans form our perceptions of others so early. The answer is that it's a primal need. There isn't typically a need to judge those people we don't expect to deal with in our lives, but for those we have to deal with frequently, we need to know as soon as possible what kind of people they are. Our minds won't be completely at ease if we spend a lot of time with people we don't feel we know.

If you disagree about this, it's because it usually happens subconsciously. It is certainly more noticeable in small children. Many children won't be their usual selves when they are with

32 *Chapter 2*

strangers. They may show apparent uneasiness. Some may want to run away. Some may even cry.

Of course, we don't like being uneasy, and we want to relax our minds, the sooner the better. To speed up the process, we'll subconsciously pay more attention to virtually everything about others that helps us know them better. We may put all of our senses into efficient use in order to see and hear better. We'll be able to obtain more information from our observations during this period.

As a result, the perception formation process won't last very long. Once we have acquired "sufficient" information and interpreted it to our satisfaction, our perceptions of other people will take shape. We won't know that we've only received a small portion of the information needed to form an accurate perception. We won't know that we've probably formed our opinions too early.

It follows that there will be no need for us to remain in an "alert" state. We'll adjust ourselves accordingly and feel more normal. We'll believe that we know others well. We'll interact with them in a manner suitable to our perceptions of them.

The Formation of Perception   33

Because it depends on many factors, the exact pace of the perception formation process can vary considerably. The first step of the process is the formation of the first impression. After we form our first impressions of others, it usually takes some time for the initially formed impressions to solidify.

During the solidification process, if what constitutes the first impressions is observed repeatedly, we'll certainly form our perceptions of others based on the first impressions. It could take just hours or days for the first impressions to add up, causing us to form our perceptions of others within a matter of hours or days. If it takes three months for the first impressions to accumulate, we may need three months to form our perceptions of others.

It is rare, however, for the solidifying phase of the perception formation process to be stretched too long. Our primal need is to form our perceptions as soon as possible. If we can't obtain enough correct information to form correct perceptions, we'll acquire enough questionable information—without our awareness—to form questionable perceptions of others.

It's also possible that our subsequent observations of others won't support our first impressions of them. In such cases, we may modify our first impressions and form our final perceptions of them differently.

But that doesn't always happen, especially if what creates our first impression of another person is overly striking. In order to make others perceive you correctly, it's best to be consistent in the impression that you make.

In his book, *The First 90 Days: Critical Success Strategies for New Leaders at All Levels*, leadership expert Michael Watkins demonstrates that the first three months in a new job is the critical period determining whether a leader will succeed or fail. If you build momentum in this period, you'll be more likely to create a virtuous cycle and gain leverage on the job. If you fail to create a virtuous cycle and establish your credibility during this period, you may later face an uphill battle.

According to numerous case studies of business leaders who either succeeded or failed in their new positions, how they started was a critical factor determining how effective they were in their jobs.

Studies also show that people coming from outside are more liable to fail than are people

The Formation of Perception   35

promoted from within. Why is this? An important reason is that while outsiders have to start from scratch in shaping the needed perceptions of themselves, those being promoted from within already have the needed perceptions of them established in the organization.

Jack Welch, the legendary former CEO of GE, often talks about how he was able to distinguish himself from others in his career. When he joined GE as a junior chemical engineer, he knew it was crucial to do well from the beginning in order to be noticed. He always looked for ways to achieve results early and to present his work successfully.

According to him, he was trying to set himself apart from his peers early. Whenever he was promoted to a new position, he always aimed for speed and achieving results early. As a result, he quickly rose through the ranks of the company and, in just twelve years, became vice president of GE.

Having experienced it firsthand, and knowing how important it is to act early, after his retirement as CEO of GE for two decades, he regrets that he wasn't fast enough when he was at GE. He wishes that he had achieved everything at an even faster pace.

Chapter 2

Perhaps the legend of Liang Zhuge can best demonstrate the importance of early impact. Zhuge was a great statesperson and general in the Three Kingdoms Period of China about eighteen hundred years ago. He was appointed prime minister and commander in chief of the Shu Kingdom at age twenty-seven. A scholar living in the countryside, Zhuge had no experience leading or governing prior to the appointment. For that reason, many people questioned whether the appointment was a wise decision. They were literately waiting for him to fail.

Other factors also made his job challenging. The Shu army was in a terrible shape at that time. For a while, they were losing one battle after another, and were chased around by enemy forces. Yet, shortly after taking the position, Zhuge was able to bring three significant victories to the Shu army.

How did he do it? He knew how to use fire as a weapon, which made a decisive difference in each of the three battles. After those victories, he completely turned the situation around. What's more, no one ever again questioned his ability, even when he occasionally made mistakes. He remained as prime minister and commander in chief until the day he died. From this legend, an

The Formation of Perception   37

old Chinese saying was also born: "A new leader must use fire three times without delay."

Hopefully you have a good start in your job and are doing well in your position. If not, there are still things you can do to make others take a new look at you. We'll discuss this more in the last chapter of the book.

PERSONALITY MATTERS

There is a good reason that personality matters to perception. As we just discussed, perception forms early because people weigh information received initially much more heavily than information received later. Research has shown that the primitive brain is mainly doing the assessment of others in the beginning. The more advanced analytical brain is largely idle at the outset. This is especially true when people acquire their first impressions of others.

The primitive brain is instinctive and reactive. We don't have to use the primitive brain consciously. It operates automatically, rapidly, and easily. Some of its main duties are seeing to our safety, likes, dislikes, feelings, and spontaneous responses. When we meet others, our primitive brains will quickly pick up information that has

38 *Chapter 2*

to do with these things. Such information has nothing or little to do with their competency, but it has a lot to do with their personality traits.

What's more, others' personality traits don't just affect our spontaneous responses in our primitive brains. They can also have an impact on how we perceive them in our more advanced analytical brains.

If the spontaneous responses in our primitive brains are positive, we will be more likely to perceive others well. On the other hand, if the spontaneous responses in our primitive brains are less positive, we may not perceive them as well.

Therefore, having a productive personality is extremely important. At the very least, your personality shouldn't be counterproductive.

THE THREE ESSENTIAL QUALITIES

Other than personality, your competency is another component shaping people's perception of you, unless you have such an overwhelming personality that the sheer force of your personality alone will do the job for you.

The personality component is about who you are. It can tell others a lot about your emotional

The Formation of Perception   39

intelligence. The competency component is about your expertise and ability—the real substance inside you. Your education, your professional knowledge, and your skills on the job are all part of the second component. Both personality and competency matter, so you will want to pay attention to both components.

Are there specific qualities that matter to perception? Since as early as the time of Aristotle over two thousand years ago, many people have studied the qualities that are most important to perception. As you can imagine, many qualities have been identified. However, closer examination of these qualities reveals that they eventually converge to form three key qualities: expertise, goodwill, and dynamism. You must demonstrate the three qualities in order to be perceived in the most desirable way.

Expertise is about your competency and your value to your job. It's important to demonstrate that you are knowledgeable, have the ability to do your job effectively, and can deliver satisfactory results.

Goodwill has to do with your personality. Friendliness, thoughtfulness, fairness, good attitude, and commitment are all part of what goodwill is about. People will often link your

Chapter 2

goodwill with virtue and integrity. In order to be regarded well, it's important to show that you respect others, have others' interests in mind, and are committed to doing a great job.

Dynamism is another quality that has to do with your personality traits. It's about being lively, vigorous, and strong. Dynamism gives your personality spirit. It will give you a presence and make you influential. It shows that you have confidence in yourself and are committed to what you believe. Whatever you do, when you exhibit dynamism, it will increase your visibility. It can even create sensation, charisma, and charm.

In essence, goodwill is the soft side of your personality. Incomplete by itself, it needs to be balanced. Dynamism, the harder side of your personality, can complement and balance your goodwill.

This balances the yin and yang in your personality. According to an ancient Chinese philosophy, yin and yang are opposite yet complementary forces that coexist in all matters. Yin can't exist without yang, nor can yang exist without yin. Both yin and yang are required for anything to be complete.

The Formation of Perception   41

In order for a person to be a complete, successful being, it is imperative that the right balance of yin and yang be incorporated in his or her personality. Here, yin is having sufficient goodwill, and yang is having sufficient dynamism. When you balance proper amounts of each in your personality, you'll be most effective in society.

Therefore, it's important to show that you are a decent person who also has a competent personality. If you only have goodwill toward others, your goodwill might not look natural or real, and others might not appreciate it as much as they should. Dynamism can make others believe that your goodwill is real. They'll appreciate your goodwill a lot more as a result.

Dynamism is also needed to make others believe in your competency. It'll make you look competent, and it can effectively help you convince others. Even if you have sufficient competency, almost certainly you won't appear to be competent enough if you don't demonstrate sufficient dynamism. Remember that no matter how competent you are, if you don't appear to be competent enough, others may not believe that you are. You need dynamism to help you demonstrate your competency successfully.

Because it can magically make you look trustworthy, dynamism is a wondrous quality. This is the most important benefit you will receive when you demonstrate dynamism.

But keep in mind that dynamism alone means little. In order to generate its positive effect, it has to be demonstrated in conjunction with your expertise or goodwill. For that reason, some psychologists have argued that dynamism should be considered an intensifier rather than a quality on its own. It's quite an accurate description of its function.

For the same reason, it's also important to demonstrate dynamism naturally and properly. If you demonstrate only dynamism, or too much of it, it won't look natural, and it can actually be counterproductive. Your dynamism has to look real in order for it to work its magic. We will discuss this more in later chapters.

THE NEGATIVITY EFFECT

Numerous psychological studies show that people tend to attach much more significance to negative information than to positive information of equal significance. In other words, negative information has a much stronger influence

The Formation of Perception 43

on perception than does positive information of equal intensity. This phenomenon is called "negativity effect."

Because of the negativity effect, failure prevention must be taken seriously, especially when striving to perform early, because early impact weighs disproportionately more than later impact.

If you are ready and know what you are doing, it is best to take charge early on in your job. On the other hand, if you still need to learn more, or if the situation isn't right for you to jump into too quickly, it's much wiser to be a little slower.

Just don't be too slow when you do so. Be sure that you learn the ropes as fast as you can so that you can still take charge and generate positive effect reasonably early.

THE FUNDAMENTAL ATTRIBUTION ERROR

The "fundamental attribution error" is a unique thing behind every aspect of the perception formation process. It refers to the fact that when we make judgments of others, we usually disproportionately attribute more of what has occurred to personal factors than to situational or external factors. This is especially true in negative situations.

In fact, very often people can't see the situational factor at all. For example, if someone looks irritated, people may not see what has made him or her angry. They may only think that this is a bad-mannered person, although anyone in the same situation may become equally irritated.

As another example, if you make a mistake at work, your boss may not see the situational factor causing you to make the mistake. Your boss may only see that you have made the mistake, and think you alone are the cause of it.

The ultimate form of the fundamental attribution error is that people tend to categorize others into various types of people. People tend to assume that everything others do is determined by the kind of people they are. It can make people doubt others and their motivation without any evidence.

Therefore, be mindful of the fundamental attribution error. Although it's a simple error, its consequences aren't. You don't want people to categorize and treat you as a questionable type of person.

The Formation of Perception 45

PRESENTATION IS EVERYTHING

As you can see, the way people form their perceptions of others is an efficient yet questionable process. It's not a scientific process designed to be accurate. Usually people's perceptions of others are only partially derived from actual observation, and the reasoning leading to the perceptions can be quite problematic.

As a result, others' perception of you can be anything if you just let everything happen on its own. To prevent that situation from happening, rather than leaving things to chance, it's best to present yourself purposefully. This will make sure that others perceive you correctly. You shouldn't just go to the workplace and see how it goes.

In order to present yourself in the most effective way, it helps to see it as a performance. Imagine that you are actively performing and telling a good story of you. The goal of the performance is to be your best, to bring out your best, and to be most effective.

Of course, your performance at work should not be just pure performance. Everything has to be genuine at the same time. The point we are making is that when you see your job as a per-

46 *Chapter 2*

formance, you'll do it better, and it will be much more rewarding. You will do more of the right things and do them more effectively when you perform.

Many preeminent experts have advocated this approach. Among them, social psychologist Edward Jones called it "strategic self-presentation." In his book, *Interpersonal Perception*, there is an extensive discussion on what it is, as well as how to make it work.

Perhaps the best way to illustrate the power of performance is to look at stars in the entertainment industry. How do actors and performers make it look so easy to become celebrities? An important reason is that they are 100 percent performing in their jobs, and the public can only see their performances for the most part. Their jobs, by definition, are to perform, which makes them look much more fascinating than they typically are.

Leslie Moonves, president and CEO of CBS, openly admits that he has benefited tremendously from his early acting career. He says that it has made it much easier for him to perform the way he needs to, and it has made a big difference in his effectiveness in his job.

The Formation of Perception   47

A great thing about this approach is that it will also stimulate your growth and expand your capacity at the same time. When you make efforts to perform, not only will you do everything much better and be regarded much better, but you'll indeed become much better.

The reason is that performing naturally requires you to do everything in the best way possible. It will help you discover your talents, and you'll be more likely to put your talents to effective use when you perform. You might have certain exceptional talents that you rarely use, don't use well, or weren't even aware of previously. When you seek ways to perform at your best, you'll be more likely to discover and effectively utilize those talents. As a result, the performance will help you bring out your best and be your best.

In order to perform successfully, be sure that you know what to actually perform, and what you want to accomplish up front—the rest of the book will focus on that. If you are prepared and can see your performance beforehand, you'll be more likely to perform effectively, and your performance will certainly be more successful.

In essence, being successful is not only about how good you should be or whether you are

Chapter 2

good enough, but also about whether you will perform well and use your talent successfully. Often it's not how good you are or what you can do that matters most. How effectively you actually perform is what usually counts more.

PART II

IMPLEMENT THE PRINCIPLES

3

ACQUIRING DYNAMISM

Be Confident

As you already know, dynamism is one of the three key qualities that you must demonstrate in order to make people perceive you in the best way possible. For that purpose, the most important thing to do well is to exude confidence in your daily activities. Your apparent confidence in yourself is essentially required for you to project a successful image.

"The man who has confidence in himself gains the confidence of others," says an old maxim. Ralph Waldo Emerson, the well-known American essayist, poet, and philosopher, put it

52   *Chapter 3*

another way: "If I have lost confidence in myself, I have the universe against me."

Confidence is the most essential ingredient in dynamism. Without it, there will be no dynamism. Confidence is what generates exuberance in you. It's what brings liveliness into your spirit. It's the vital force that makes you look vibrant.

With confidence, you'll appear to know more, you'll appear to be stronger, and you'll be more highly regarded. With confidence, you are essentially conveying a message that you are truthful, trustworthy, and influential.

The words you say may not always reach others, but your confident voice will always be heard clearly. The knowledge you have may not always empower you, but your apparent confidence does. Whatever you do, your confidence will always speak up for you.

In a beauty contest, your confidence will make you look more beautiful. In a boxing match, your confidence will make you appear stronger. In debate, your confidence will make you appear more convincing. There is no occasion where confidence doesn't work to your advantage.

Referring back to the Three Kingdoms Period of China, Liang Zhuge, the commander in chief

Acquiring Dynamism

who used fire to defeat enemy forces three times in a row, also demonstrated that merely exhibiting confidence was powerful enough to stop attacks from enemy forces.

In a fierce battle with the Wei Kingdom army, led by General Yi Sima, due to a fatal mistake committed by a high-level commander of his, Zhuge suddenly found that the enemy troops were rapidly approaching the city where he was staying. Zhuge had few soldiers with him. It was too late for him to run away, and it would be futile to fight. It was a desperate situation.

In order to stop the enemy, Zhuge decided to try a daring tactic. He ordered the city gate opened and the few soldiers removed from the defense positions. Then, with his face overlooking the enemy force, he sat down on top of the city wall over the city gate and began to play the pipa (a musical instrument like a guitar). Zhuge knew that if he demonstrated confidence, Sima might suspect that the Shu army had set a trap, and the Wei army might not dare to advance into the city.

Sima, another well-known general at that time, knew that the key to figuring out what was going on with the Shu army was to observe Zhuge's every move. Sima knew that the

Chapter 3

subtle clues would lie in Zhuge's face and body language.

Watching not too far away from the city gate, Sima deployed all his senses to determine whether there was any uneasiness in Zhuge's face or in the way he played music. Seeing no sign of uneasiness and hearing no discord in the melody of Zhuge's music, Sima indeed concluded that Zhuge must have set up an ambush inside the city.

As a result, Sima ordered his army to withdraw. By demonstrating confidence, Zhuge saved the city and avoided a humiliating defeat in such a precarious situation.

Animals also know that confidence represents strength when assessing other animals. In a television program about animals in the wild, an animal expert demonstrated that a confident appearance alone is sufficient in overpowering a huge polar bear.

In the ice-covered Arctic, the animal expert carried no weapon and made no movement to scare the polar bear. He merely stood with a calm and confident appearance. Yet it was powerful enough to make the polar bear keep a distance from him. In fact, the polar bear actually

Acquiring Dynamism 55

appeared to be nervous. It was an amazing display of the power of confidence.

At work, in order to do your job effectively, it's vital that you communicate effectively with others. There are several things that matter critically to your effectiveness in communication. Whether you project confidence is one of them.

When you speak, not only are you communicating the message in your words, but you are also telling others whether they should believe you. When you speak, others will pay attention to your nonverbal expressions, such as voice volume, tonality, facial expressions, eyeball movements, and gestures. Through these observations, people will be able to tell whether you have confidence in what you are saying, and whether you are committed to it.

This often occurs without people's knowledge of it. Rarely do we just use our analytical brains to judge others. Our primitive brains are almost always involved in the process. In order to make others truly hear what you are saying, it's important to first satisfy the needs of their primitive brains.

The primitive brain can only process body language and other nonverbal expressions,

56   *Chapter 3*

which usually reflect a lot of your confidence level. When you exude sufficient confidence, it activates others' primitive brains, and their analytical brains will therefore want to hear you. This makes your confidence level matter critically to your effectiveness in communication.

Quite often, even when people don't understand your verbal message, as long as they can sense your confidence in your nonverbal expressions, it will be sufficient for them to believe you and accept your message. For those who don't need to understand your verbal message, they may not even bother to process your message in their analytical brains.

Confidence can even make you look attractive. If you use any physical standard to measure the beauty index of exciting people, you will find that many of them are far from perfect. For many of them, their confidence is what makes them appealing. When you exude confidence, your eyes will radiate light, your faces will be luminous, and you will be irresistible to people's hearts. Confidence is the best makeup.

Confidence can also bring out pleasant emotional responses in others. First, when you show confidence, it will at least relax others' minds. Your confident appearance will naturally make

Acquiring Dynamism

you look like an authentic, trustworthy person, which can easily put other people at ease. Second, others may see your confidence level as an indication of your attitude toward them. With confidence, you'll be more likely to appear enthusiastic, and others will be more likely to respond with enthusiasm. This will help you connect effectively with other people.

What's more, when you demonstrate confidence and show an upbeat spirit, you are essentially expecting or demanding positive responses from others. This will help bring out cooperative responses from other people. If you demonstrate your belief in yourself, and you believe others will feel the same about you, it can powerfully condition others to respond positively toward you. People often respond the way you appear to be expecting them to.

For those who are doing well in virtually all areas of society, one of their common characteristics is that they often exhibit sufficient confidence. Do they exude more confidence than they actually have? Yes, many people do. In her book, *Executive Charisma*, leadership expert Debra Benton writes, "The truth about CEOs worldwide is that about 99.9 percent exude more confidence than they really have." It's important

58   *Chapter 3*

to demonstrate confidence in order to do your job effectively and to be successful.

Of course, when you exhibit confidence, be sure you don't overdo it. If you exude too much confidence, others may think that you are arrogant or trying to inflate yourself, and it may actually damage others' perception of you. Overconfidence almost never works.

Overall, if you want to gain the confidence of others, it's vital to demonstrate first that you have confidence in yourself. Demonstrating confidence allows you to acquire dynamism and be effective. Be sure that you exude confidence in whatever you say or do. If confidence is already a personality trait of yours, even better.

BE COMMITTED

Like confidence, commitment is another critical quality that you need in order to demonstrate dynamism effectively. Commitment will strengthen your character and bestow you a strong personality.

Commitment is not simply about working hard and being dedicated to your job. That's only part of it. Commitment also means that you are dedicated to what you believe, you are deter-

Acquiring Dynamism

mined to implement it, and you are going to do whatever is necessary to achieve the results.

Why does commitment matter so much to your dynamism? First, because your level of commitment is also an indication of your confidence level. As we discussed in the last section, confidence matters a great deal to others' perception of you. You can have all the confidence in the world, but without commitment, others may not necessarily see you as a confident person.

Your confidence has to be visible to add value to others' perception of you, and your commitment is always required to make your confidence visible and believable. If you are clearly committed to what you believe, others will be more likely to believe that you have sufficient confidence in yourself. Confidence and commitment go hand in hand. It's vital to escort your confidence with commitment.

For example, let's say you have a great proposal to make. If you want to convince others that it's a great proposal, be committed to it. Otherwise, you may appear unsure about your proposal and lacking the needed knowledge, even if you actually know more than everyone else does on the subject.

60   *Chapter 3*

Remember, what matters is not only how good you really are, but also how good you appear to be. If you aren't committed enough, you may not seem believable, and both you and your proposal may not be seen as valuable. If you withdraw your proposal when you meet resistance, it may even appear that you are admitting your proposal is not good enough, or that you are wrong, regardless of whether those things are true or not. People can't read your mind. Often it's what you appear to be that is more believable to others.

Moreover, your level of commitment also tells others how firm you are. It conveys to others whether you truly mean what you are saying or doing, and how competent you really are. While your confidence can make you look strong, your commitment can make you look even stronger. It can thereby strengthen your dynamism effectively.

You already know that your body language will tell others whether you have confidence in yourself, but that's not all it does. Your body language will also tell others whether you are committed to what you are saying.

For that reason, commitment can give you amazing power in communication. If you stick

Acquiring Dynamism

with what you are saying and show your commitment to it, not only will others see you as more believable, but they'll also see you as stronger and more influential.

As a result, being committed can make you a strong person and a real player at work. When you are committed, others will sense your inner strength and take you more seriously, and you'll be more effective when working with others. This will make a significant difference in your career prospects.

For that very reason, you may decrease your chances of career success if you aren't committed enough. Your expertise alone is not good enough to ensure success in your career. Without commitment, chances are good that you won't be considered competent and taken seriously.

This is not to say that your expertise isn't important, but that you need to be committed to make your expertise useful. At work, it's not always the most knowledgeable people who excel. Those who are most committed to what they are doing are usually the ones who achieve more. They don't typically think about excuses as to why the job can't be done successfully. Instead, they'll do whatever is necessary to get the job done and achieve the results. It matters not only to their own success, but also to the success of their organizations.

Therefore, organizations pay attention to candidates' level of commitment when they hire people, especially for important positions. A few years ago, the company I worked for needed to hire a midlevel manager from outside. The company interviewed many candidates for the position. Although most showed sufficient knowledge for the job, many of them couldn't show that they had the required level of commitment. They failed to show that they would effectively sell and push through their agendas. When asked how they would influence others in various departments to get the job done, some candidates even said that it was up to others. This is the main reason many candidates failed their interviews.

As you can see, whether you are committed to what you are doing and to what you believe matters critically to both your character and what you can achieve. Your commitment will always increase your effectiveness. It will make you strong and give you influence. In order to achieve career success, it's vitally important to demonstrate commitment.

TAKE ACTION

The third element necessary to demonstrate dynamism effectively is action. You shouldn't just demonstrate dynamism when you speak. Rather, it's important to demonstrate it essentially all the time.

The function of action is that it will generate energy within you and make you look dynamic. It's the most effective expression of passion. It's spirit in its most lively form. If you are constantly in action, you'll naturally look vibrant, enthusiastic, and full of life. Action is the ultimate form of dynamism.

At first glance, this might seem puzzling because action should consume energy and therefore make people look less vigorous. But the opposite is actually true. Action can activate the body and make it function at the maximum level. It can be compared to turning on the engine of a vehicle. The engine does burn gas, but it also produces energy for the vehicle to run. Energy promotes energy.

You already know the importance of confidence and commitment. The most effective way to demonstrate them is by taking action. Without sufficient action, others may not see you as

64 *Chapter 3*

confident and committed. In fact, until you take action, your confidence or commitment means little. Only when you take sufficient action can your confidence and commitment be real, and be seen as real.

At work, if you take insufficient action or wait too long to take action, it can make others doubt you. They may assume that you either lack confidence or aren't committed to the job.

As it's often said, "The road to hell is paved with good intentions." People don't have the ability to know others' intentions without seeing action. In order to express your intentions effectively, be proactive and take sufficient action. Demonstrate with action that you are a competent player and will make a difference.

OVERCOME BARRIERS

Start with the Problems

For many of us, it's not that we don't want to take action. Often we are just slow in doing so because certain irrational yet plausible thoughts are holding us back.

The first barrier is that you might see problems as obstacles. You might think subcon-

Acquiring Dynamism   65

sciously that certain problems have to be solved first in order for you to take action. You might see that the situation is not satisfactory enough. You might see that you don't have everything you need. If you think that everything has to be satisfactory in order to take action, you will always find reasons why you should wait rather than taking immediate action.

However, it's neither essential nor realistic that everything has to be satisfactory in order to take action. It's best to view problems as opportunities. Then, you won't see problems. Instead, you will see there are plenty of good opportunities, and you will find enough reasons to take action.

It will make a big difference in your effectiveness when you focus on what can be done to solve problems, or how a job can be done despite the problems. With this approach, you'll see that problems present opportunities. Indeed, problems are reasons to take action. They can make us valuable and useful.

Do What Can Be Done

When you take action, don't wait until you have come up with a super idea. Your idea doesn't have to be flawless. It doesn't have to solve all the problems. It's okay to start with an idea that is less than perfect, as long as it addresses the problem you want to solve, or can help you understand the problem, thereby helping you come up with a better idea.

Quite often action can lead you from small ideas to much bigger ideas. Ideas that you don't have when you are waiting can fly to mind after you take action, and opportunities that are invisible when you are hanging around can become noticeable once you are actively seeking ways to achieve the best results.

The reason is that action can stimulate your mind to think, to generate ideas, and to catch opportunities. Action can make you ready to take more actions, bigger actions, and better actions. It can make you more alert and able to see things that you may never be able to see otherwise. Once you take action, you'll be able to find effective ways of making up for the inefficiencies of your current approach, and you'll be able to get the job done to your satisfaction.

Beat Uncertainty

Lastly, when you take action, don't let the fear of possible negative consequences hold you back, whether it is fear of rejection, fear of criti-

Acquiring Dynamism   67

cism, fear of failure, or fear of other what-ifs. Fear creates fear. It's important to fear less in order to take effective action.

At work, as in life, it is typical that you'll often face uncertainties and unknowns. If you have to feel certain about the outcome in order to take action, you may always find yourself lagging behind. If you hesitate too much and take too much time taking the initiative, you may never be effective at work, and you may never be seen as competent, regardless of how knowledgeable you actually are.

In addition, when you take action, don't concern yourself with others' negative comments. Even if you have a superb action plan, you might still hear discouraging comments. Don't let others easily stop you. Otherwise, you will encourage them to stop you even more afterward, and it will make it even harder for you to take effective action in the future. Be sure that you stand your ground, take action, and do all that is necessary to execute the job well. That will open the path to less resistance or opposition in the future.

Therefore, don't let anything hold you back. Whatever uncertainty you face, it's only a possibility that it's uncertain. However, it can become a real thing and truly stop you if you worry about it too much. As President Franklin D. Roosevelt said in his first inaugural address, "The only thing we have to fear is fear itself."

The most effective way to deal with uncertainty is to face it firmly and take action in spite of it. This will allow you to beat uncertainty and expand your opportunities. If you take the initiative and step forward in spite of the uncertainty, you'll see that you can make things happen and get the job done. Then you will become more effective in your job, and your confidence level will increase.

4

DELIVERING RESULTS

DELIVER RESULTS EARLY AND CONSISTENTLY

It's important to deliver results early because perception forms early. When you do your job, others will be watching and judging you at the same time. If you don't deliver decent results early enough, others may form a questionable perception of you before you finally deliver the results. Then, when you finally get the job done, they may be reluctant to change their perception of you. Delivering results early will help you avoid the problem.

It's also necessary to deliver results consistently in order to build your credibility. Good

70   *Chapter 4*

perception needs to be maintained, which requires you to demonstrate your effectiveness on a steady basis. That will make your efforts truly count.

If you only make one good shot in the beginning, the impact will fade away eventually. If you only make a good shot every now and then, others may think the results were accidental. Either way, if you don't deliver sufficient results, it may not add much value to others' perception of you.

Therefore, be sure to deliver results both early and consistently. This is the most productive way to deliver results, and it should be your guideline when doing your job.

WORK ON ACHIEVABLE TASKS

An effective way to deliver results early and consistently is to work on achievable tasks. When you initiate a task at work, weigh seriously the achievability of the task. If it requires a lot of investment or a tremendous effort, think about it carefully before diving into the work.

As you already know, personal factors weigh disproportionately more than situational factors when people judge others. If you work

Delivering Results

on a tough task and can't deliver results early, rather than realizing that you are working on a challenging task, others may only see that you haven't delivered results, or that you are struggling on the job, and they will tend to think that you aren't good enough for the job.

Every year there are junior professors who have to resign their positions because they haven't shown that they can be accomplished experts in their fields. For many of them, it's not that they lack the ability or haven't made enough effort. The problem is that they have selected tasks that are too challenging. They have ambitious ideas, but precisely because of that, they can't execute them easily. They can't deliver quick results to demonstrate their abilities and potential.

Likewise, every year there are new executives who are forced to leave their organizations. They've tried to implement great plans, but time flies and their great plans have not produced the expected results. Consequently, before their plans are completely implemented, or before enough time has been given for their plans to produce results, the organizations have lost confidence in both the plans and the new executives.

At a meeting I attended many years ago, a highly accomplished authority talked about how

Chapter 4

to deliver results productively. He said that it's best to start with an achievable idea and get the job done well. Then you start another achievable idea and again execute it successfully. When you deliver results consistently, you'll project an effective image of yourself, and others will be more likely to think you are capable. That will lay a solid foundation for you to tackle tasks that are more challenging.

Even many Nobel Prize-winning geniuses spend most of their time working on achievable tasks. For many of them, an important reason for their success is not that they are more talented or possess greater ability, but that they have successfully struck a balance between the complexity and achievability of what they are doing.

At work, quite often the excellence of the implementation of your idea is what matters more. When you work on achievable tasks, it'll allow you to optimize the process and deliver the best results. It's much better than barely making a challenging idea work. Idea itself doesn't count. It's what you actually deliver that matters more.

Therefore, whatever you want to do, whether it can generate results within a reasonable period should be an important measure of its value. The

Delivering Results

best idea is not necessarily the grandest idea. If your plan is too challenging, come up with something else that is more achievable. This is especially important if you've just joined an organization or have just started your career.

What should you do if you have a super idea that you really want to try? First, be sure that you have considered not only the reward of success, but also the complexity and the risk associated with it. If you still think it's worthwhile to pursue the idea, convince your boss first. If your boss supports you, you are truly blessed and should do whatever it takes to execute it well. If your boss shows hesitation, try again to get him or her on board. Sometimes it can be difficult for others to see what you want to achieve as clearly as you do. Maybe your boss will agree the next time you bring it up.

However, if your boss is clearly not interested, work on something else instead. Without your boss's support, it can be very difficult for you to do the job well. Besides, you may also damage your relationship with your boss if you don't listen to him or her.

If you find that you have underestimated the difficulty of your current task, it's important to know when to fold. Don't feel that it is a dif-

74   *Chapter 4*

ficult thing to back away from it. Otherwise, it might put you in an even more difficult position if you continue not making progress. The longer you wait, the harder it is to rid yourself of the task, which may result in more damaging consequences.

Sometimes it can be emotionally difficult to cut the work from your mind, even if it is wasting your talent, time and energy. However, it's important to make the tough call and move on to the next thing if your task is clearly going nowhere.

Overall, whatever you do, be sure to strike a good balance between achievability and complexity. On the one hand, be sure that you are bold enough. On the other hand, be sure that you are sensible at the same time. When you balance it well, it'll be much easier to deliver results, and you'll have more fun at work.

Always remember that it's best to promise less and deliver more. It's much better than the other way around.

BUILD ON STRENGTHS AND SUCCESS

Another way to ensure that you'll deliver results early and consistently is to work on your

Delivering Results

strengths and build success on the successes you've already accomplished. With this approach, you'll minimize the amount of trial and error in your efforts, your tasks will be more achievable, and you'll be able to deliver adequate results. It is a proven formula for career success.

Therefore, when you do your job, find your strengths and utilize them intensively to accomplish something early. If it works, do more of it and do it even better. It's not a good idea to put the results aside and start from scratch for something else. Don't think that you should keep exploring so that you can find an even better starting point—you can do so, but don't use all your resources to do it. It's much better to first establish a base and grow from there than to keep wandering around.

When your approach is to build success on success, it will also make it easier for others to accept and support your approach. At work, it's not typically easy to convince your colleagues or your boss to accept a brand-new proposal. However, if your proposal is based on what has already been successful, it can effectively help you convince others to accept it, and it will be much easier to win their cooperation.

76   *Chapter 4*

Of course, it's also important that you don't just repeat the process mechanically. Be sure that you also consider how to expand your strengths and add more value to the successes you've already achieved. This way, you are still utilizing your strengths and still building success on success, but you are also increasing your strengths and enlarging the successes. This will be more exciting, more rewarding, and more fulfilling.

FOCUS ON PRIORITY

Whether or not you can focus on priorities is another important factor determining how effective you can be in your job. In order to deliver results early and consistently, it's crucial that you focus on high-priority tasks.

You don't have too much time allotted at work, and you simply can't do too many things or handle too much pressure on your shoulders. When the pressure is tolerable or acceptable, it can make you more productive. But if you have too much to do, it will actually be counterproductive. You may make more mistakes in your job, your mind's sharpness may be reduced, and your stamina may decrease. While you can work very hard, you won't necessarily achieve good results.

Delivering Results

At work, almost certainly there are enough tasks to keep you busy throughout the day every day. If you don't think what to focus on, it's very easy to be sidetracked by less important tasks and put the important tasks on the back burner. Consequently, you may not spend enough time on the right things and may have difficulty achieving satisfactory results in your job, even if your important tasks are achievable.

You might think that you should finish less important tasks first so that you can focus all of your time and energy on more important tasks afterward. Although this may seem to be a reasonable thought, it doesn't actually work, for you'll never finish less important tasks. With this approach, you'll always see less important things first, and you'll always find yourself working on everything but the most important tasks. We see what we are looking for. If you think that you should get less important things done first, you'll always see these things in front of you.

Likewise, when you think that you should work on high-priority tasks first, that is where your attention will be focused, and the distracting low-priority tasks will occupy little or no space in your mind. Over time, it can even

78   *Chapter 4*

become a habit to work on high-priority tasks first.

That is the reason some people are more effective than others are. While two people can be doing exactly the same job, they might fill their minds with two very different agendas. One might be all about the high-priority tasks, while the other might be distracted by less important activities and thoughts.

In order to focus well, be sure to avoid initiating more than you can handle effectively, even if they are all important tasks. Otherwise, you may find yourself struggling to do all the jobs. While it's easy to initiate all the tasks you want to do, it usually requires a lot more effort to actually get them done.

RESULT-ORIENTED LEARNING

At work, your job is to deliver results. Whether or not you've learned what you need to learn, it's always important to deliver results early and consistently. For that reason, effective learning is a necessity. Only by learning quickly can you demonstrate your competency effectively.

For the same reason, systematic learning, which is the way we are taught in school, is not

Delivering Results

the best way to learn at work. Although thorough, it is too slow to meet the needs of most workplaces.

It's most effective to learn the most needed knowledge first. This way the learning task is result oriented, and what you learn can instantly help you do your job. In contrast to systematic learning, in which you lay the foundation first and build knowledge one brick a time, result-oriented learning encourages you to first acquire the most needed knowledge and use the knowledge early.

For example, to use the remote control of your new TV, you don't have to study how the remote control is wired. As long as you've learned the function of each button on the remote control, it's good enough.

Of course, if you still want to learn the details of how the remote control works, you can do so. But never reverse the learning sequence, because you don't want to wait a week or a month to actually use the remote control. You do want to enjoy your new TV right away, don't you?

It's often said that knowledge is power. Although the statement is true, it's often misunderstood. Knowledge alone doesn't guarantee success. Instead, whether you can use your knowledge effectively is what determines the outcome. Being effective at work is not really about how knowledgeable you should be, but about whether you can effectively apply your knowledge and achieve satisfactory results. Knowledge alone is never enough.

Therefore, to reiterate, be sure that you learn the most needed knowledge first. When you begin to work on anything new, you may see or encounter things that are unknown to you, and you'll naturally have a sense of what you need to learn first. An effective way to learn is to imagine that what you need to learn is a remote control. Study the functions of the buttons first, get familiar with them, and become comfortable pressing them. This will ensure that you can perform well right from the beginning.

Then, once you can perform competently in your job, take the initiative to learn the essential fundamentals. It's important that you don't just learn superficially. There are things you must comprehend thoroughly in order to do your job even better. Do allocate some time to learn the important fundamentals.

With this result-oriented approach, whatever new knowledge you learn, it can help you do your

Delivering Results   81

job right away. What's more, you can also learn more effectively with this approach. Knowledge is such a thing that you haven't truly learned it until you've utilized it effectively. Using what you've learned is an effective way to retain what you've learned.

At work, one thing for sure is that you won't be able to learn and know everything. If you think that you should comprehend everything thoroughly, you may spend too much time learning, and you may get burned out long before you've finished your learning task. Accept the fact that you won't be able to learn everything. This will help you find smarter, more effective ways to learn and do your job.

What's more, when you focus on using knowledge rather than learning knowledge, not only will you learn better, but you can even create new knowledge about what you are doing. Then others will think you are more knowledgeable and will want to learn from you.

DELIVER EMOTIONAL RESULTS

Whether you've delivered emotional results can make a big difference in how your work will be received and where your work may end up. It

82   *Chapter 4*

can also make a big difference in how others will evaluate your performance on the job.

As we discussed earlier, the mind doesn't always work in a scientific, objective manner. The emotional brain often has a huge influence on what the analytical brain sees and how it reasons. The emotional brain functions like a control button. If the emotional brain is pleased, the analytical brain will tend to see positive things and reason positively. If the emotional brain is displeased, the analytical brain will tend to see negative things and reason negatively.

Therefore, other than making sure that you deliver results early and consistently, it's also important to deliver the results in a manner that elicits positive emotional responses.

In order to do so successfully, try to work on tasks that matter most to your boss. This will help you create an emotional bond with him or her. With that bond in place, you'll be supported more on the job, and the results you deliver will also be better recognized. Even if you don't think that your boss's idea is the best, be sure that you still do your best to implement it.

Another important thing is to be in charge of something. Psychological studies show that

Delivering Results

people tend to see whoever is in charge as more capable than others are. Of course, whatever you are in charge of, be sure that you do it well and deliver satisfactory results.

Even if you aren't in charge of anything, it's still important to keep yourself visible on the job. You don't have to keep talking all the time—which isn't always productive anyway. But it's important to express your opinion convincingly on a regular basis. At least it shouldn't be surprising to see you speaking out. When you keep yourself visible, it will help you project an active, capable, and effective image. You'll be noticed more and get better recognition as a result.

It's also a good idea to work on things at the next level. When you do so, the emotional brain will weigh these things disproportionately heavier. If you keep doing so, almost certainly you'll be perceived as more talented and more capable than others are.

This also applics to everything else in society. The value of your talent is often measured by what you are doing and how people perceive it. If you are doing what people believe to be more important, you will be regarded as more talented and more capable.

Chapter 4

It doesn't necessarily require more effort or more talent to tackle tasks at the next level. The key is to step forward and take the initiative. It's important to mentally put yourself at the next level. Once you stand higher, you'll see everything differently, and it will help you identify tasks that are more rewarding.

After you get the job done, it's also important to package and present your work effectively so that it does elicit the right emotional responses eventually. Be sure to give your work an pleasant personality and make the results look appealing. It can make a big difference in others' perceptions of both you and your work.

For example, when companies sell their products to consumers, they design and use attractive packages to catch consumers' attention and trigger the right emotional responses. They know that having produced the product is only part of the job, and it's also important to package and present the product in an attractive fashion.

When you present your work, don't assume the final results are the only things that are important, and don't make it look too simple. If you present the results casually and don't have much to say about the work, others may assume that you are careless on the job, they may doubt

Delivering Results 85

the quality of your work, and they'll be more likely to look for problems in your work. Simplicity is supposed to be good, but if it looks too simple, it may actually be counterproductive.

Likewise, when you write a report or proposal, don't make it look too simple either. It's true that the appearance of your report and its content are two different things. Nevertheless, if your report appears to be inadequate, others may not take it seriously, and it will be more likely to be ignored. It's important to make it look adequate and inviting.

In his book, *On Writing Well*, author William Zinsser says that he appreciates plain language and values plain writing. But he also acknowledges that plain writing isn't the norm in most corporations. "Managers at every level are prisoners of the notion that a simple style reflects a simple mind," says Zinsser. While people's emotional needs are often irrational, we can't ignore them.

DELIVER A COMPETENT YOU

Lastly, when delivering results, be sure to deliver a competent you at the same time. If you only do the job itself competently, but can't

Chapter 4

demonstrate that you yourself are competent enough, others' perception of you may not be as good as it should be.

Don't assume that your work alone will speak for itself or for you. It's important to be competent enough to speak up successfully for your work, which is often the only way to make others pay sufficient attention to it.

Therefore, other than business tasks, pay sufficient attention to personal growth tasks. Be sure to make your personal growth one of your most important focuses.

It's vital to identify what you need to do for your personal growth and work on it persistently. For example, you may need to acquire more knowledge and become more skilled in your field. Or you may need to improve your communication and interpersonal skills. In order to be successful, it's important that you have sufficient competency in these areas.

In addition, pay attention to what the successful people at the workplace are usually talking about. These are often issues that matter most to the success of the business. Learn as fast as you can to make yourself a competent player at talking about the same topics. This

Delivering Results

will sharpen your competitive edge substantially in your job.

It's important that you don't keep postponing working on your personal growth tasks, and that you work on it persistently. Once you have done so and developed strong "muscles," you'll become stronger and more competitive. You will then have a much better chance of excelling in your career.

5

COMMUNICATION

THE ROLE OF COMMUNICATION

In order to demonstrate your expertise, good-will, and dynamism effectively, it's important to communicate well. As you already know, how good you really are and how you are perceived can be quite different. Others can perceive you as better than you really are, more or less as good as you really are, or not as good as you really are. The outcome often has a lot to do with how you communicate with others.

In an important sense, communication is the real clothes a person wears. Communication can decorate you, glorify you, and promote

Communication 89

you. Communication can also misrepresent you, distort you, and conceal you. Depending on whether or not you communicate effectively with others, communication can either elevate you up or pull you down.

THE CHALLENGE OF COMMUNICATION

An often-overlooked thing about communication is that you can't choose whether to communicate with others. You are communicating with others when you talk actively or listen attentively. The communication is still occurring when you sit there doing nothing. As long as you are with others, there will be communication going on.

For example, if you sit in a meeting and don't say anything, others might infer by your silence that you aren't interested in the matter, don't know much about it, or have nothing to contribute. It could certainly be that none of these inferences are true, but people can't see what is inside you. They have to make assumptions—and they do so in a way that makes the most sense to them.

Because you can't stop communicating and are actually communicating with others all the time, rather than letting communication take its own course, it's best to be in charge of what you communicate and be in control of its content.

In order to do so effectively, it's important to speak out, although communication is much more than just words. Speaking out is a necessity. You have to be heard. You have to be visible.

As far as speaking effectively goes, different ways of saying the same words can produce vastly different results. In order to make others truly hear what you are saying, it's important to speak in a convincing way.

The reason is that no language is accurate enough. Your words aren't necessarily going to be understood in the way you intend. When you say anything, it can almost certainly be understood differently from what you really mean.

More importantly, other than the words you speak, you are also communicating with your body language. Your eyes, facial expression, gestures, and tonality are all sending out information to others. How you say what you say also carries meaning, and it often matters even more than the actual words.

Why is body language so powerful? Because no one has to think about it to understand it

Communication 91

instantly. Our primitive brains will do the job automatically and more than adequately. Although we humans may not comprehend others' verbal messages correctly, we typically have no doubt that we will read and comprehend their body language accurately.

This is the reason it's so important to speak assertively and make your body language click with your verbal language. At the very least, you shouldn't let your body language unsay what you are saying in your verbal message.

Remember, there is always a close association between appearance and perception. Unless you sound or appear to be good, how good you truly are may not count as much as it should. It's vital that you speak with conviction and confidence.

BE COMMITTED TO YOUR MESSAGE

As we just discussed, when you speak, others will read between the lines. They'll make sense of your body language, and make a decision as to whether they should believe in what you are saying. In order to communicate effectively, your body language and your verbal language must synchronize with each other.

Chapter 5

However, it will be quite a burden to your mind if, while speaking, you also have to think about your body language. It will likely be too much for your mind to handle so many things simultaneously. You also risk losing focus of your message if you let your mind handle so many different things all at once.

As a personal example to illustrate the challenge, I know I can't make eye contact on purpose. All communication experts believe that eye contact increases effectiveness in communication. But if I think too much about it in the middle of a conversation, my mind will be distracted. I won't be able to listen well or speak effectively.

Therefore, it's not always practical to think a lot about your body language while communicating with others. Fortunately, there is an easier, better way to fix the body language in order to speak convincingly. You actually just need to be committed to your message when you speak. Your commitment will generate sufficient force in your words and automatically make you speak assertively. This will help a great deal when communicating with others.

When you are committed to your message, all the pieces of your assertive body language will

Communication 93

automatically piece together on its own. This way you can still focus on what you are saying. Your mind won't be distracted when you focus on your message. It's obviously a more practical, better way to make your verbal and nonverbal message in harmony.

Once you are committed to what you believe, the naturally formed assertive body language will also fit you perfectly. Your body language should be a true, intrinsic part of you. When your assertive body language looks natural and genuine, what you say will certainly be most believable.

Therefore, being assertive doesn't necessarily mean that you have to turn up your volume or make certain gestures. You can still be who you really are. You can still be yourself. Just make sure that you are committed to your message. As long as you are determined to get your message across, your body language will look fine, and your message will be heard.

A prerequisite for this approach is that you do know what you are talking about. When you know the topic well, you will be more likely to make clear, logical, and accurate points, and your commitment to your message will generate even better results.

For that reason, don't say anything unless you sure know what you are saying. Likewise, don't say anything that matters little. Since you are unlikely to commit yourself to those things, you may not speak assertively when you talk about them. If you aren't committed to what you are saying, your actual body language may even be the opposite of what you want it to be. It can even cause other people to take you less seriously when you speak about important things later.

To achieve the best results, be sure that you have a real opinion on what you want to talk about. Don't let others see that you don't have your own opinion or are afraid to express your opinion. In order to be most effective, it's important to have an opinion and do have something valuable to say.

In addition, be sure that you make clear, unambiguous points in your message. Whatever you want to say, focus on the main points, and don't say that it's both good and bad. You may think that you should express your opinion honestly, or that your message should be comprehensive. However, that will only reduce the effectiveness of your message, for it will appear to others that you are unsure of what you are

Communication
95

saying and aren't committed to it. If your words contain uncertainty or ambiguity, others won't take what you say seriously, no matter how truthful you are.

In particular, if anyone disagrees and challenges you on what you are saying, be sure that you stand your ground and have no hesitation to defend what you believe in. When you defend yourself successfully, others will pay even more attention when you speak.

It's also important to demonstrate your commitment to your message by selling it persistently. If you are only good at debating, but not good at pushing your agenda forward and implementing it, you aren't really committed to it. Once others know that you are only good at talking, they won't take your words seriously, and what you say will be more likely to get lost as a result.

Sometimes people may not make obvious objections to what you want to do. Nevertheless, it doesn't mean that they'll accept it and cooperate with you later. Be sure to keep pushing the agenda forward, and follow up on it constantly until the job is done. It's best to be a proactive communicator. Don't simply assume that everything will be taken care of automatically.

Chapter 5

After considering all of this, you might still say, "Maybe it's not such a good idea to be so committed. After all, I am not sure whether the results will be satisfactory." It's true that commitment won't guarantee the results. Nevertheless, it's definitely the best way to increase your chances of success, both for each individual task and for your career as a whole. It's much better than regretting that you did not give it your best shot.

Of course, being committed to your message doesn't mean that you shouldn't listen to what others are saying. If what others say is correct, you can and should agree with them about their opinions. When you take this approach, others will be more likely to collaborate with you, and you will be even more effective in your job.

BE PREPARED WITH YOUR MESSAGE

In order to be committed to your message so that you can speak with confidence and conviction, it's important that you know the issues well and do have good points to make. When you firmly believe in your message, your commitment will be absolutely the right thing to do, and your body language will be most convincing.

Communication

The most reliable way to know your message well and have a firm belief in it is to be prepared. Preparation is the best guarantee. Once you are prepared, it will be much easier to speak with confidence and conviction.

It's especially important to be prepared for meetings. Since there is usually more than one attendee at any meeting, and the discussion is also more comprehensive, you might look particularly inadequate if you aren't prepared in advance. For the same reason, if you perform well in meetings, the positive impact will also be significant.

Even if you don't plan to say anything in a meeting, it's still a good idea to be prepared. This will make you a good listener and keep you engaged. If what you hear in the meeting doesn't seem right to you, because you have done your homework, you can be confident in knowing that you'll ask the right questions.

When you prepare your message, examine your argument carefully and make sure it's a solid one. You should comprehend both its pros and cons. Make sure that the pros weigh much more than the cons, and that the cons are not fatal.

98   *Chapter 5*

It's important to be prepared for every meeting. If you are only prepared every now and then, others will be more likely to remember the times that you were inadequately prepared and had less satisfactory performances—due to negativity effect. It's persistent performance that counts.

Once you've done it persistently for a while, it will become much easier to continue doing so. You may initially have to spend quite a bit of time preparing, but soon you'll be able to do it in much less time. What you have learned each time you prepare will accumulate, thereby helping you prepare afterward.

What's more, all the preparation will help you do your job better and better. In the end, not only will you communicate more effectively, but you'll also do much better at many other aspects of your job, such as thinking critically, problem solving, coordinating work, and delivering results.

Furthermore, when you've prepared well for each meeting, you'll become more knowledgeable and more influential, and you'll enjoy your job more and more. It's almost certain that eventually your heartbeat will be in synchronization with the heartbeat of the entire project, the

Communication

entire division, or the entire organization. You'll therefore be highly effective in your job.

DELIVER A GREAT PRESENTATION

Are there mysterious qualities that you have to possess in order to deliver a great presentation? The most enduring theory about presentation came from Aristotle. He said that each presentation consists of three things: the content of the presentation, the audience, and the speaker. All three components have to be taken care of in order to have a successful presentation.

First, for the content of the presentation, there must be substance. It has to be solid, and it has to make good sense.

Second, as far as the audience is concerned, it's important to keep their attention during your presentation. Quite often, the content alone is not sufficient to ensure a satisfactory presentation. You may have to deliver emotional satisfaction and make the presentation exciting to the audience.

Therefore, be sure that you know as much about the audience as possible. Who are they? What do they want to know? How can you keep them engaged with the presentation? When you present what the audience wants to know, you'll be more likely to keep their attention, and they'll be more likely to enjoy and appreciate your presentation.

As the speaker, you are the third component of your presentation. The audience's perception of you will have a significant impact on what they'll hear and see in your presentation. In each presentation you give, you are always part of what you are presenting. The better you present yourself, the more likely your presentation will be successful.

The best way to work on the three components is preparation. As we discussed earlier in this section, preparation can make you more effective in communication. Considering presentation is an even more important communication event, it's crucial that you prepare for your presentation. Preparation can help make you your best.

Your mind is extremely powerful, but it needs to be organized and trained in order to perform superbly. To deliver a great speech or presentation, you may have to speak nonstop for half an hour or even longer, and you have to be punchy and to the point. It's a tremendous demand for the mind to come up with concrete words one by

Communication   101

one in a logical manner for so long. It's therefore important to be prepared.

President Ronald Reagan was a great communicator. An often-cited episode of him was his answer to a question about his age in his reelection debate with Walter Mondale. He replied, "I will not make age an issue of this campaign. I am not going to exploit for political purposes my opponent's youth and inexperience." It was such a powerful answer that even Mondale had no choice but to laugh. After that, no one asked the question again and the age issue disappeared completely in the campaign.

But it wasn't a response that suddenly appeared in Reagan's head when the question was asked. According to Roger Ailes, his election consultant, Reagan prepared the answer in advance because one of the issues of the election was whether he was too old to serve another term. Reagan knew someone might ask that in the debate.

Franklin D. Roosevelt was another great presidential communicator. During his four-term presidency, he made twenty-seven well-received Sunday evening radio addresses to American people. According to Grace Tully, his secretary, the ritual that preceded each broadcast always included days of intense preparation, and FDR would practice the address many times until he was satisfied.

The reason I mention these presidential episodes is to illustrate that deep down we are all the same, and no one is made of special material. Everyone has the ability to deliver great presentations. However, in order to do so successfully, it's important to be prepared.

When you prepare your presentation, be sure to think how to capture the audience's attention from the start. Because the audience is virtually completely with you and wondering what you are going to say in the beginning, it is necessary to deliver something that will satisfy their expectations and get their attention early on. If you can do so, you will have a much better chance of keeping the audience engaged with your presentation.

For this very reason, while it is a good idea to start your presentation with an introduction, don't drag it on too long. Otherwise, you may lose your audience before you finish the introduction. Even if you don't lose them, it will still stimulate generation of negative thoughts about your presentation.

Communication 103

Likewise, try to end your presentation with a strong closing. During the process of compiling all of the components of your presentation, allocate some exciting or important information to the ending. This will make the ending an exciting point of your presentation. It can therefore effectively increase the impact.

Another important aspect of the preparation is to anticipate likely questions and have answers prepared for them, as in the earlier example of President Reagan. You don't want to be caught off guard.

Not only does the president of the country do so before meeting the media, but attorneys also do it before fighting in court. Likewise, sports coaches work out beforehand the measures for all possible scenarios of their games. When they have already thought about everything that could happen in a game and are prepared, they will be more likely to respond correctly to each situation during the game.

To anticipate likely questions your audience may ask, again, first examine the interests of the audience. What do they know more about? What do they care about most? People tend to ask questions about those things that interest them most.

104   *Chapter 5*

Second, examine the content of your presentation. Anything in your presentation can trigger a question from the audience. If anything is potentially problematic or hard to comprehend, your audience may ask questions about it.

As the speaker, you will want to demonstrate sufficient expertise, goodwill, and dynamism during the presentation. Be sure you know the subject well and have the essential knowledge. If there's anything that you don't fully understand, work on it right away. It's important to let the audience see you as knowledgeable and believable.

Lastly, it's a good idea to practice your presentation for a number of times until you've become comfortable with it. This will make the final delivery of your presentation smooth and enjoyable to the audience.

Once you've prepared well, you'll be ready to deliver your presentation successfully. You may even find that the actual delivery of your presentation is surprisingly easy.

Avoid Unnecessary Debate

At work, one thing you can't avoid is that others may disagree with you, or that you may

Communication 105

disagree with others. As a result, debate is often inevitable. However, it's still best to avoid unnecessary debate. If you can achieve the same thing without debate, why bother debating? Before we discuss how to debate effectively, let's first discuss what you can do to minimize the chances of unnecessary debate.

Suppose you have a proposal to make. It's a good idea that you first show the reason you are proposing it before showing all its details. If you put forth all the details at the outset, chances are good that others will not think along the same lines. They may not listen to you attentively, and they will be more likely to disagree with you.

There are two reasons causing the problem. First, we all want to know why someone is proposing something. If you don't first say anything about what you want to achieve, others may make assumptions about it, and they may make incorrect assumptions.

Second, others may have their own ideas of what should be done, and they'll immediately see the difference between what you are proposing and what they think is the right thing to do. Since most people believe their own ideas are better, they'll be more likely to think that your proposal is not as good.

Chapter 5

Therefore, instead of directly focusing on what exactly you plan to do, it's best to first focus on why you want to do it, and what you want to achieve. When you focus on the reason, others may see that they share the same goal as you, even if they have different ideas about how to achieve it.

With this approach, your communication will be less about convincing others to see what you've seen, for you are letting them know that you've seen what they've seen. When they eventually realize that you merely have a different idea about how to get the same job done, it will still be much easier for them to accept it because you've already turned on their positive thinking modes.

Even if others see that you want to achieve a different goal, it's usually not as easy to find problems with the goal as it is to find problems with the details. It's always a good idea to talk more about the reason, but less about the details.

What if you have to reveal many of the details, and you know others may have problems with them? After presenting the reason for your proposal, it's a good idea to ask whether anyone disagrees with you about the reason before

Communication 107

showing them the details. That will minimize the chances of debating with them when you do get to the details.

Likewise, if you have good results to share with others, it's best that you show the results before showing how you've achieved them, at least briefly. This way, others will be much less likely to look for problems in your work.

President Bill Clinton is credited as being good at connecting with the American people. One reason is that he seldom told them much about the details of what he wanted to do, but he would say a lot about why it was important. It was a most effective way of soliciting support.

Another way to avoid unnecessary debate is to minimize your unnecessary negative remarks about what others are saying or doing. If you have to make comments about others' ideas, simply give positive comments about those things with which you agree. You just need to say what points are good. It's unnecessary to make clear what you disagree with, unless it is something you shouldn't ignore and think you have to point out.

This won't compromise the effectiveness of your words. Although you haven't touched the

108   *Chapter 5*

things you disagree about, it is equally clear that you have a different opinion about those things. No one can argue with you that you haven't made a positive comment about a particular point of his or hers. It's a most effective way of avoiding unnecessary debate while making your point equally clear at the same time.

In addition, don't reject an idea unless it has a fatal problem or you have a better idea. It's always easy to be negative. However, it's not always easy to come up with truly good ideas. Don't dismiss another's idea simply because it's not perfect.

If you have to contest something, focus only on what you really disagree about. At work, sometimes a small disagreement can make people argue about everything and reject whatever others say. When that happens, the discussion or debate will likely go sour.

Having discussed the reasons to minimize your unnecessary negative remarks, I want to emphasize that those reasons shouldn't be just guidelines to help you conduct yourself. They are also arguments with which to arm yourself if others make meaningless negative remarks about what you are saying or doing.

Excel in Debate

Although you should minimize your unnecessary negative remarks, if you do see a serious problem in what others are doing or saying, don't hesitate to point it out. Likewise, if you have an idea in which you firmly believe, it's important to sell it persuasively. In either case, if anyone questions what you think is right, stand your ground and defend yourself effectively.

In order to debate successfully, you need skill and debate know-how. The fact that you are right doesn't necessarily guarantee that you'll carry the day in the end. In debate, you may have to wrestle with tricky arguments. If you have difficulty defending yourself against such arguments, it may appear to others that you are wrong or that there are holes in your argument, regardless of whether it's true. Even if you are entirely correct, debate can kill your ideas if you fail to do it well.

As always, unless you appear to be good or correct, how good or how correct you truly are might not count as much as it should. The outcome of debate is determined not only by who is right or by who represents more truth, but also by who is smarter and has more wits. As you al-

110   *Chapter 5*

ready know, intelligence often overpowers truth
in debate.

In order to debate successfully, an important
thing to remember is that when others challenge
you with a question, you don't have to reply to
exactly what is asked. Instead, find a way to continue getting your message across. This way, no
matter how tough the question is, you can be
sure it won't create problems for you. What's
more, you can turn it into an opportunity to
keep making your case.

Whatever message you are selling, others may
see the pros, the still uncertain aspects, and the
cons about it. Accordingly, the questions others
ask can be categorized into three types. The first
type asks you to clarify the pros, the second type
asks you about the uncertain aspects, and the
third type asks you to address the cons.

For the first type of questions, answer them
directly. These questions provide the easiest opportunity for you to keep selling your message.
Be sure to put these opportunities into effective
use. Make sure that you speak with confidence
and conviction.

For questions asking you to address the uncertain aspects of what you are selling, don't di-

Communication 111

rectly say that you don't know the answer, even if you truly don't know. Otherwise, it may make you appear inadequate, as if you don't really know the subject well. In the end, others won't remember the question, regardless of what it is—whether it's a difficult question or a meaningless question. They will only remember that you couldn't answer it.

What you can do is explain why it's difficult to know the answer, and why the point you are making is still valid. Or you can ask, "What do you really want to know by asking that question? I'll be able to answer your question better if I know why you are asking that." Alternatively, you can find a problem with the question, and question the question.

These are all effective ways of handling such questions. When you say more than "I don't know," even though you won't truly have answered the question, it will still appear that you have answered it well—in fact, you do have.

As for questions asking you to address the cons of what you are selling, you don't have to answer the questions directly, unless the raised concerns are invalid and can be easily dismissed. It's vitally important that you don't step into the weak area of what you are advocating.

Chapter 5

If you acknowledge that there are problems in your proposal, however insignificant they might be, those problems may become real issues and get all the attention in the debate. This could trigger others to question the problems even more. Consequently, you might find yourself in the hot seat. Why? First, because you can't keep admitting the problems—only a fool would advocate anything riddled with problems. Second, it will be difficult for you to dismiss the problems after you've already admitted them. You may find it hard to talk yourself out of your dilemma. It'll make yourself vulnerable.

On the other hand, you don't have to dismiss hostile questions directly. The reason is that what is questioned may be real, although the problem may not be that significant. If you dismiss these questions directly, it may appear that you are ignoring the truth.

An effective way to address those questions is to answer them indirectly. You can reiterate the benefits of what you are selling. If you demonstrate that the benefits are more important and are worth pursuing, it will be a good way to answer these questions. With this approach, you can still talk positively and confidently when you address these questions, and you will

Communication 113

still be in control of the situation. It may even appear that those questions shouldn't have been asked.

It's true that it's not a perfect way to address the questions, but you may have to do so in order to stand your ground successfully. People often won't be satisfied that others give in just a little bit. They tend to want others to give in completely. It's important to be result oriented. Don't help others defeat you.

Therefore, I must reiterate that it is vital that you don't touch the weak area, or problem, of what you are advocating. If others frequently bring up a topic that you can't avoid any longer, try asking a few rhetorical questions about the valuable aspects of what you are advocating. As you know, a rhetorical question is not meant to be answered. It is to assert more emphatically what you are advocating. It is what others can't dismiss. Asking rhetorical questions is an effective way of handling the situation.

To show its usefulness, I want you to recall what President George W. Bush does when he is challenged about the war in Iraq. He'll frequently ask rhetorical questions to stand his ground: "Isn't it better that Saddam is out of power and is in jail?" "Isn't democracy better

Chapter 5

than dictatorship?" "Isn't it better to fight the war against terrorism on enemy soil?" Whether we like it or not, he is able to stand his ground successfully by asking these powerful rhetorical questions.

In order to debate successfully, it's also important to recognize tricky tactics in others' arguments. Sometimes people don't just come up with valid arguments in debate. Intentionally or unintentionally, they may also utilize various logical fallacies that may look like valid arguments. These fallacies may even appear reasonable and powerful enough to change the outcome of the debate.

In such cases, you must recognize the fallacy immediately, point it out, and make it invalid. Don't answer the fallacious question directly. Just make it clear that it's an erroneous argument. It'll be an effective way to address it.

Of course, this is not the place to have a comprehensive discussion of all the logical fallacies. If you want to learn more about them, you can find many books devoted to the topic. But we will look at some of the most common ones that you might encounter at work. Be sure to be familiar with these fallacies so that you can recognize them immediately.

Communication   115

One of the most used logical fallacies is exaggeration of what you are saying. Through exaggeration, others can twist what you've said to a degree that it's no longer what you mean but is still linked to what you've said. As a result, what you've said may appear worthless and be dismissed easily.

This fallacious practice is often termed "straw man argument," for it's like setting up a straw man, inserting an exaggerated version of your argument into the straw man's mouth, and then criticizing the straw man for being unrealistic. By fabricating an unreasonable argument and attributing it to you, your opponent can easily make your real argument appear unfeasible and can thereby dismiss it with ease.

Let's say that Tom has proposed something at work. Even if he has proposed doing just one thing, David can say that Tom has proposed fifty or a hundred things to do, and that it will take many people a long time to get the job done. If Tom doesn't point out that David has exaggerated what he is saying, others may believe that Tom has indeed proposed something out of the realm of common sense. It can be hard for others to realize that David has distorted what Tom is saying.

116   *Chapter 5*

If anyone exaggerates what you are saying, it's important that you recognize it immediately. Otherwise, it might create an even bigger problem for you, for the straw man might make you defend the exaggerated argument, leaving you confused and helpless in the debate.

Therefore, be sure to point out directly that your idea has been exaggerated or twisted, and the opposing argument is thereby invalid. If you just say that it's not what you meant, or it's not what you have said, you may not draw enough attention to your opponent's misleading argument. To other people, it may even appear that you are flip-flopping or denying what you just said. It's crucial to point out the fallacy directly so that others can really see the problem, and you can invalidate the opposing argument effectively.

A fallacious argument that is in some ways similar to the straw man argument is called a "slippery slope argument." It also involves using exaggeration in the opposing argument. A slippery slope argument says that doing what you are saying will make certain undesirable things unavoidable. It's thus better not to implement it, or the consequences can be chaotic or disastrous.

Communication 117

While doing what you say doesn't necessarily mean that the claimed undesirable consequences will follow, the slippery slope argument can make it appear that it will indeed set off the unwanted events and create a mess.

For example, suppose Tom proposes a market rollout plan for a new product. David might state that there are many more products to be launched, and the rollout plan will create a chaotic situation because the company doesn't have the resources to do it all. At first glance, it might seem that Tom hasn't thought about his rollout plan thoroughly. But the fact is, all the products won't be launched at the same time, and the rollout plan won't overwhelm the capacity of the company. Besides, there is no rule that all the products have to be launched in exactly the same way.

As a second example, let's say that Tom makes another proposal at work. David can make it appear that everything else has to be halted and all other important things will derail if Tom's proposal is implemented. A slippery slope argument can be used to dismiss virtually anything.

If you find anyone using the slippery slope argument to extrapolate the consequences of your proposal, state that there is no inevitability that

Chapter 5

the claimed consequences will follow, and the argument is therefore invalid.

You may also encounter logical fallacies that bring other things or other people into the debate. Let's say that you've just made a proposal. Someone opposing your proposal might say that the job has never been done in your proposed manner, or that it has always been done in a particular manner. You may also hear that no other company has done it that way, or that someone who is an authority won't think it is a good idea and no one will buy into it.

This type of fallacy can appear in various forms. What they have in common is that they are all trying to move the focus to things that don't really matter. The focus should be on the pros and cons of the proposal. If an argument is about things that don't matter, the argument is irrelevant to the discussion.

It's important to recognize the fallacy and point out that it's an irrelevant argument. Although all these arguments are fallacious intrinsically, the claims in each argument may be true, and the argument can thus appear to be legitimate. If you don't point out the problem and make the argument invalid, you may appear to be out of touch with the world.

Communication   119

A somewhat similar logical fallacy is bringing up what you've said or done in the past. Your opponent may say that what you are advocating now is what you previously opposed, or that you are now opposing something you supported before. Consequently, it might seem there is an obvious problem with you.

This is a fallacious argument because what is right or wrong should be measured within the context of each case. It's thus erroneous to mix two different things and talk about what is right or wrong for both of them. If anyone uses this fallacy in his or her argument, consider using these words to make it invalid.

An extreme version of the fallacy is questioning you instead of what you represent. For example, let's say you point out a serious problem in someone's proposal. Instead of addressing the problem directly, your opponent might say, "I'm trying to make a good proposal, but you have a problem with it. What's your motivation? Do you want to see bad results?" By attacking you personally and putting you on the hot seat, your opponent can easily avoid the real issue and get away with the problem.

You may also encounter other types of fallacies, and they can show up in various forms.

Chapter 5

However, all logical fallacies, including those not covered here, use essentially the same tactic, which is evading the real issue and targeting and making a fuss about what only appears to be the issue.

Therefore, you can counter all fallacies using the same method: pointing out clearly that the opposing argument only appears to be relevant to the real issue but is in fact irrelevant.

Should you use logical fallacies in your own arguments? Obviously, it's not a good idea to make a habit of committing fallacies in debate. As you can see from the discussion, if there is a fallacy in your argument, others may point it out, and that can put you in an uncomfortable position.

However, this doesn't mean that your argument must be absolutely fallacy free. If a fallacy is used properly, it can be a most effective way of communicating your idea and convincing others to accept your argument.

For example, in principle, all analogies are fallacies. But if an analogy is crafted well, it's a powerful way to strengthen your argument. This was another reason that President Bill Clinton was so good at connecting with the public when

Communication 121

he was in office. He was excellent at using analogies to make his point.

Nonetheless, always make sure the fallacy in your argument is proper, and you can back up your argument with solid rationale so it has no chance of boomeranging back. In other words, make sure it's not quite a fallacy.

As you can see from the discussion, debate can be both fun and demanding. While it's preferable to avoid debate, if it is necessary, go for it and don't retreat. Debate is not necessarily a bad thing. It can stimulate the generation of new ideas. It can lead to better understanding of the issue. It can even help create friendships.

KEEP YOUR COOL

Communication expert Frank Luntz once said, "Language, it's just like fire. It can either heat your home or it can burn it down." The metaphor fully conveys the importance of speaking constructively in communication. In order to communicate well, it's vitally important to keep an eye on what you say, and know what you should and shouldn't say.

Accordingly, the focus of this section will be on what you shouldn't say. While it's important to say the right thing when you should, it's even more important that you don't say the wrong thing when you shouldn't.

To achieve that, it is critical that your emotions are always under control. This will make you much less likely to say things that you may regret later.

What can make our emotions run out of control? The most common cause is misunderstanding other people. You already know that we tend to commit the fundamental attribution error. For that reason, it is very easy for us to misjudge others.

Accordingly, in order to keep your emotions under control, keep in mind that when others displease you, almost certainly there are situational reasons causing it. It may not be that they deliberately want to disagree with you. It may not be that they deliberately want to create problems for you. Don't assume that those having different opinions have a problem with you.

But what should you do if others truly do have a problem with you? What should you do if whatever you say is always attacked? What should you do if others behave poorly toward you?

Communication 123

The first thing to do is to stay calm and keep your mind peaceful. Of course, this can be challenging. Quite often, force draws another force to it instantly, and it can be easy to become enraged. But you must maintain your calm.

There are good reasons for doing so. First, keeping your cool under such circumstances will help you project a sophisticated image. Second, if you don't think that other people are behaving properly, don't commit the same behavior yourself. Otherwise, you are behaving improperly too. If you really care about how other people perceive you, it's important to be cool in all situations.

This is not to say that you should back away under such circumstances. It's just best not to overreact or behave in a counterproductive manner. You can continue talking firmly yet calmly, if the situation still permits it. When you maintain your calm, you will also be able to reason better and respond more intelligently.

Remember that whatever you say, once you've said it, there is no way to unsay it. It is vitally important to safeguard your words. You don't want to put in a lot of effort and do a superb job at work, just to see it destroyed by a few words from your own mouth.

124   *Chapter 5*

Aristotle said, "Anyone can become angry. That is easy. But to do this to the right person, to the right extent, at the right time, with the right motive, and in the right way, that is not easy." For all the reasons that we've discussed here, keep your cool.

Be a Good Listener

Obviously, communication is a two-way process, and expressing yourself well is only part of the equation. It's also important to be a good listener and comprehend what others are saying.

An important benefit of being a good listener is that it's an effective way to demonstrate your goodwill. Why? Because we all want to be listened to, we all want attention, and we all want to be understood. You can easily make others feel positive about you by being a good listener. As American physician and writer Oliver Holmes said, "It's the privilege of wisdom to listen."

It's important to recognize that others are also capable people. Once you take others seriously, it will naturally help you listen attentively to them. There is no doubt that you will learn a lot from others if you truly listen. Even if you find out that others aren't as good as you think,

Communication

you'll still benefit from listening to them, because you can be sure that you know better.

Being a good listener doesn't mean that you should always keep quiet. There is no conflict between being an assertive communicator and being a good listener. A great communicator is one who not only speaks well, but also listens with understanding and empathy.

6

RELATIONSHIP

PERCEPTION CREATES RELATIONSHIP

Perception is the foundation of relationship. Due to the force of perception, how others regard you largely determines how they will relate to you. Likewise, your perceptions of others largely determine how you will relate to them. After you interact with each other for some time, the experiences you have with each other will determine the relationships. The relationships can be good or not so good. It all depends on how you perceive each other, and what experiences you have had with each other.

Relationship 127

On the other hand, your relationships with others will also strengthen your perceptions of each other. If you have good relationships with others, they will be even more likely to see you in a positive light. If the relationships are not so good, they will certainly perceive you quite differently. Perception and relationship go hand in hand.

To make your relationships work for you, it's best to start from perception. Whatever helps others regard you as a commendable person will also help you relate to them well. Perception is the key.

TREAT YOURSELF WELL FIRST

In order to relate to others well, it can be tempting to think that you just need to be nice to them. However, it's actually critical that you first treat yourself well and have a great relationship with yourself.

This isn't to say that we shouldn't respect and treat others well. It's just that we can't be so obsessed with politeness that we allow it to hinder effective communication or even immobilize us. We also have to take good care of our own feelings and treat ourselves well at the same time.

128 *Chapter 6*

As we discussed earlier, goodwill alone is not enough for others to perceive you well. It's also necessary to demonstrate sufficient dynamism, which requires confidence in yourself and commitment to what you believe. Obviously, you can't acquire dynamism without treating yourself well first.

If you try too hard to let others see that you are polite, gentle, or friendly, they may see it as unnatural or unreal. They may even think that you are trying to use niceness as a way of manipulating them, whether or not that's your intention, and they may not want to buy into it.

In particular, be sure you speak up for yourself if others have incorrectly accused you of something. If you take the heat and don't defend yourself, others may not know that you are innocent, and they may believe that you are admitting you are wrong. It's doubtful that others will know you are simply trying to avoid conflict or take care of any other concerns, and it will negatively affect the way others view you.

If necessary, it's also important to point out what others fail to do well or have done improperly. For example, if the quality of a task at work is compromised, you must point it out. Otherwise, you are putting yourself in a position

Relationship

where you might be blamed because you failed to do what you should.

If you find it difficult to take care of everyone's feelings, telling the truth is the best way to balance all of the concerns in your mind. It is the best way to set you free. Whenever you find yourself in a dilemma between telling the truth and taking care of other concerns, it's usually better to say the truth, and say it as early as possible. This way, others will have the best chance to know you well and perceive you correctly. This is also often good for others. They may actually respect you more as a result.

Oprah Winfrey, the most influential talk show host in the United States, was once or twice late in meeting her staff a couple of years ago. A staff member didn't like it and told her directly that she was being disrespectful to them and should stop being late. As a result, it never occurred again, and she respects her staff even more.

Of course, all this is not to suggest that you be an arrogant person. Be sure that you do your best to be nice to both others and yourself. But if for any reason you can't do both at the same time, speak your mind and don't give yourself a hard time.

130   *Chapter 6*

BE OPEN AND DIRECT

In order to demonstrate dynamism effectively, other than what we already discussed, it's also important to be open and direct when interacting with others. This will make it easy for others to know you correctly.

If you are less forthright, you will almost certainly appear less confident. Consequently, you won't demonstrate sufficient dynamism, and you may appear to be lacking in strength and competency. As mentioned earlier, no one is going to spend much time trying to figure you out in order to really know you well. If others can't understand you easily, you will allow them to misunderstand you and perceive you incorrectly.

What's more, being indirect can make people wary of you. It may make them view you less positively, or even negatively. They may doubt whether they should trust you as a result.

Therefore, don't choose to be indirect for any seemly reasonable reason, whether it is to feel more comfortable or to make you look "more respectable." Instead, it's best to maximize your effectiveness by being direct. Don't let others guess what you imply. Don't be inhibited by

Relationship 131

this or that concern. Don't feel uncomfortable, guilty, or wrong for speaking your mind.

For example, if you want to ask others for something, ask both politely and directly. Don't think that others should be able to figure out what you want. If you have to imply to others about what you want, they won't like it. They may even become annoyed.

This goes as far as speaking up about what you want to accomplish in your career. If you don't reveal your true self and your needs, it's unlikely that your boss will know what to offer you.

Indeed, when looking for someone to fill a position for a particular job, other than weighing people's ability, those making the decision also take people's passion and desire for the position into consideration. If the competition is tough, which is usually the case, whether you have shown your interest often makes a big dif ference in whether you will get the position.

All this is not to say that you should tell everyone everything about yourself. It's just that you should definitely make it easy for others to know you so that they can know you correctly, and you can work with them most effectively.

SEE EACH RELATIONSHIP IN ADVANCE

Many of us are only managing our relationships with others. We deal with the relationships when we have to, and we don't think much about them the rest of the time. Often it works fine. But at the same time, we may be missing much greater relationships with others. Maybe we can handle the problems in our relationships much more effectively. Maybe we can make each relationship much more satisfying.

For that purpose, it's best to know in advance what each relationship should be, as well as how to achieve it. With that knowledge, you will know what you should do and what you should avoid in each relationship. It will help you control the events that may occur in the relationship, and the events will be less likely to dictate the relationship.

With this approach, instead of managing each relationship on a day-to-day basis, you'll be able to build it according to a plan, and you'll have a much better chance of achieving what you want from that relationship. It's much better than letting the relationship take its own course.

Therefore, be sure to think thoroughly about your relationships with others. Think what each

Relationship 133

relationship should be, and how you can accomplish it successfully. Then work on each relationship as you've envisioned. Do it proactively and persistently. When you do it well, you'll be more likely to have the type of relationship you envisioned.

To help you envision your relationships with others, next we'll discuss three important relationships in the workplace. They are your relationships with your boss, your reports, and your peers. The quality of these relationships will largely determine your effectiveness in your job.

WITH YOUR BOSS

Obviously, your supervisor determines a lot of your worth in your job and your chances of success at the workplace. Your boss's perception of you is most important to you. Your relationship with your boss matters the most to your effectiveness. If your boss regards you well, it'll be much easier for you to do well.

For that reason, it's important to take 100 percent responsibility for making your relationship with your boss a successful one. Make sure that he or she will support you in your job.

Chapter 6

Do a Great Job First

In order to relate to your boss well, most important of all, always keep in mind that your boss wants to do well in his or her position. Your boss has to deliver satisfactory results for the organization.

Your boss doesn't have the ability to do the entire job alone, however. If your boss can't do a good job and make his or her team productive, it may cause him or her many headaches. Your boss needs help, and wants you to help as much as possible.

That is where your relationship with your superior should start. Be sure to let your boss see that you've made a difference in the job, and that you've made his or her job easier. If you do your job well, you'll help your boss a lot and it will certainly be appreciated by him or her. If your boss can't count on you on the job, almost certainly you won't have a good relationship with him or her. It's important to demonstrate that you are valuable for the job.

Of course, if you want to excel at work, you may have to demonstrate that you can do even better on the job. You don't have to necessarily do more to achieve that. If you work on what

Relationship 135

is most important to the job, and you also do it successfully, your boss will certainly appreciate your work much more.

Therefore, try to work on most important tasks, and make an effort to work at the next level. Don't wait to be asked to do these tasks. Be proactive and come up with good ideas to tackle them. If you come up with a great way to achieve what your boss wants to achieve, it's unlikely that he or she won't let you do it. Your boss will be pleased to see that you want to contribute more and work on tasks that are more important.

It's imperative that you see the job the same way your boss does. If you work on what only you think is important, your boss may not appreciate your work as much as you expect.

Moreover, when you work on what matters most to the job, do whatever it takes to execute the job successfully. If you fail, your boss might not want to give you a second opportunity. It's vital to make your boss see that you are reliable.

A great thing about working on what is important to your boss is that you'll have better resources and receive more support from him

Chapter 6

or her. After all, who doesn't want to support what matters most to him or herself? This support will allow you to deliver even better results. Then, it will also make your boss feel good, for he or she has been saying that the results will be good.

Having your boss's support also means that he or she will care even more about your work. It's like an investment. The more you invest in a stock, the more it matters to you, and the more you want to see the stock rising. If your boss keeps supporting you, it will keep adding value to your relationship with your boss, and the relationship will keep being strengthened.

There is another reason you need to have sufficient support in your job. Because of the fundamental attribution error, people can be irrational and weigh personal impact disproportionately when compared to situational impact. If you fail to do your job well because of insufficient support, instead of seeing the real cause, others may question your competency on the job.

So don't just wait for your supervisor to give you support. If you need anything, ask for it. Don't let your boss see that you don't really need him or her. You might think that your boss

Relationship 137

would appreciate your being independent, but that's not often the case. Many people want to feel needed and want to help others, unless too much is asked, or asked too frequently.

At work, your effort and your boss's support are two essential ingredients in ensuring that you do well. When the two ingredients add up, it will help you not only deliver great results in your job, but also build rapport and trust with your boss.

It's also important that while you work on your boss's priorities, you still be creative on the job. If you just follow your boss mechanically, he or she may not value you as much as you expect. In order to maximize your value, be sure that you demonstrate creativity.

But always keep your boss informed about what you are doing. If what you want to do might surprise your boss, talk to him or her before starting the work. Otherwise, your boss might feel that you have kept him or her on the outside, which might make you appear untrustworthy.

In particular, let your boss know when there is a problem. If it is going to take significant time for you to solve the problem, or if it's so big that you can't handle it on your own, inform your boss as early as possible. Don't keep waiting, because the longer you wait, the more difficult it is to inform him or her.

When your supervisor knows the problems you have to solve, and the effort you are putting into the job, you will be more likely to receive the credit you deserve for your contributions. Otherwise, even if you have worked very hard to achieve the results, your boss may think your job is easier than it is. If the results you deliver are unsatisfactory, he or she may even believe that you haven't made enough effort on the job.

Just don't bring every problem to your boss, because that will make you look both inadequate and annoying. If a problem is not difficult to handle, you don't have to inform your boss immediately. Instead, work on the problem and get it fixed as soon as possible.

Overall, if your boss relies heavily on you to do the job and sees that you can't be replaced easily, he or she will certainly value you highly.

Respect Your Boss

We all want to be respected, but that need is especially strong for someone who is in charge.

Relationship 139

Accordingly, other than doing a great job in your position, it's also important to demonstrate respect and loyalty toward your supervisor. When you do so, you can strengthen your relationship with your boss even further.

This, of course, means that you shouldn't say or do anything to upset your boss. If, for instance, your supervisor is making a particular point in a meeting, don't say anything that undermines his or her efforts. Try your best not to argue with your boss, particularly publicly.

If you have differences with your boss, be sure that you do see what your boss sees. If you still think that you are right, and it's too important not to speak up, talk to your boss again. You may see that he or she will agree with you the second or the third time you talk about it.

If your superior has any concerns for what you want to do, it's important that you take them seriously and come back with a convincing solution, even if you don't think the concerns are valid. When you make your case again, your boss will almost certainly want to know whether you've addressed his or her concerns. If you show that you've listened and done so, he or she will be more likely to be receptive to your opinion and thereby consider it again. If your boss sees that you haven't addressed the concerns, it might be the end of the entire process.

In particular, don't disagree with your boss repeatedly. If your boss often has difficulty seeing what you see, or vice versa, consider looking for another position in the firm, or a different job altogether.

If you frequently disagree with your boss, he or she is certainly going to see you as a problem, even if you are always right. As we've said many times in this book, unless you appear to be good, how good you truly are may not matter as much as it should. If you often have disagreements with your boss, i.e., if you often appear to be wrong to your boss, it's only natural that it will negatively affect his or her perception of you. Even if you always turn out to be right, the outcome may still be the same because your boss will feel bad about it. You can be as sincere as possible, but your superior may still view you quite differently. This will eventually cause your relationship with your boss to go sour.

In the reality TV show *The Apprentice*, whenever a team member disagrees frequently with the project manager, the project manager always sees the team member as a problem. If the team loses the contest, the project manager

Relationship 141

always blames the team member who disagreed frequently, no matter what the real cause of the loss was. It's not accidental that it has occurred repeatedly in the show.

Of course, it's vital that you don't diminish yourself while showing respect for your boss. Otherwise, your boss may not respect you as much as he or she should. Be sure you are always self-assured while showing others respect.

This goes as far as politely clarifying any misunderstanding your superior may have about you. If your boss is in any way disrespectful to you, let him or her know that it is improper. Only when your boss also respects you can you have a truly healthy relationship with each other.

WITH YOUR REPORTS

Your relationship with your reports is another important relationship that has to function well in order for you to be effective. If you can't lead or manage them effectively, it's unlikely you will be able to do your job successfully.

Act Like a Boss

Your title alone is not sufficient for you to lead effectively. In order to be an effective boss, it's also important to act like a boss. That will help your reports perceive you and accept you as their superior.

There is always a close association between appearance and perception. If you don't act like a boss, your reports may not truly accept you as their boss. That will make it difficult for you to lead successfully, and you may not be an effective superior as a result.

Don't assume that your expertise will automatically make you an effective boss. It helps, but it doesn't guarantee it. What matters is not only how good or how qualified you really are, but also how good or how qualified you appear to be.

This requires you, of course, to demonstrate confidence in yourself and be committed to what you say and do. Be open, direct, and assertive when you interact with your subordinates. This way, all the verbal and nonverbal signals that you send them will be coherent and convincing.

It's also important to act decisively when you interact with your reports. If you hesitate too much, if you look unsure, or if you change your mind too frequently, you may confuse them.

Relationship   143

Worse, they may not take what you say seriously, and you won't be seen as an effective boss.

Therefore, don't change your mind too quickly about anything you have said. Even if you are not sure about the results, it is still important to be decisive, so long as you believe it is the best way to accomplish what you are setting out to do. Don't let your reports suspect that you don't have confidence in what you want to do, or that you aren't committed to it. If you demonstrate confidence and conviction when you speak, they will be more likely to believe and accept what you are saying, and they will be more likely to do their jobs well.

This is not to say that you shouldn't be sensible and have to make quick decisions all the time. If you aren't ready to make a decision, let your reports know that you need more time to think about it. Then, once you have made your decision, be sure it's executed well before you try something else or move to the next stage.

It's also important to keep your cool. Your job won't always go as well as you want it to. Failures, errors, disagreements, and various other problems are essentially unavoidable. When a problem occurs, keep your cool, and don't automatically make instant assumptions about it.

Chapter 6

This will allow you to think more clearly and therefore handle the situation more productively. If you simply assume that your subordinates are the problem and blame them for everything, it won't help solve the problem. It can make the situation even worse.

As always, be sure that you are a good listener. At first glance, it might not seem that a good listener fits well the image of an effective boss. However, the opposite is actually true. Being a good listener will make you appear full of goodwill. It will help your reports feel that you respect and value them. What's more, being a good listener will help you learn important information and make correct decisions.

In order to make it work, it's also important to know when to do what, and balance everything we just discussed. Whenever possible, ask questions and listen attentively first. If you need to know more, ask more questions and listen more. Then, once you believe you have sufficient information, make your decision, be committed to it, and make sure that it is executed well.

Be Result Oriented

At work, your job is to deliver satisfactory results for the organization. If you can't do so,

Relationship 145

eventually you may find yourself in trouble. For that reason, your relationship with your reports has to help you deliver good results, and you have to make your relationship with your reports result oriented. Don't worry whether you'll be liked by your reports or whether you'll be popular to them. Otherwise, you may not be an effective boss, and they may not really respect you.

In fact, being result oriented can serve as the foundation for building a great relationship with your reports. It can ensure that your relationship with them is healthy, genuine, and long lasting.

It's best that you have the right people. If your reports will take the initiative to achieve great results, they will certainly do the job well. But regardless of whether you think you have the best reports, there is no doubt that the majority of your reports typically want to and can do well on the job. Most people want to demonstrate that they have the talent and are valuable for what they are doing. In order to achieve great results, it's best to harvest results from their desire to do well at work.

For that purpose, whenever possible, let your reports get more involved with what they are

Chapter 6

doing, and be sure they can wield influence over the decisions on the job. When they see there is no limit on what they can contribute, they'll be more likely to pour their hearts into the job, and they'll want to go the extra mile to do it well.

For example, if a problem has to be solved, ask your reports for ideas, and work out the solution with them. Unless necessary, don't directly tell them how they should do the job.

It will make a big difference in your reports' passion for the job when they can use their talents fully. Whenever possible, delegate tasks to them and let them take the lead. Let them see that they matter a lot to the job. You don't want them to feel that they are undervalued or underused.

This naturally means that you shouldn't micromanage your reports. Whenever possible, focus on the results, and give them enough elbow room to achieve the results. It can be quite discouraging if you micromanage your reports, and they have to do everything exactly your way. If you bother them too much, you may even make it difficult for them to do the job.

In particular, always keep in mind that your job is not to criticize or punish them, but to sup-

Relationship 147

port them and make it easy for them to do well on the job. Unless there is an attitude problem that you have to address, being indiscriminately negative and critical is not typically productive. Don't hurt your reports' enthusiasm for the job.

In fact, if you want them to be most productive on the job, you have to speak up for them and let them see that you care about them and are fair to them. When you speak up for them and give them credit, they will be much more likely to see you as someone worth working for, and they will want to do the job even better.

Just don't overdo it when you praise your reports and speak up for them. Only praise those things done truly well. If your reports receive your praise too easily, it's unlikely that they'll appreciate it. Whenever you praise them, be sure that you truly mean it.

Using these approaches, you aren't managing your reports. You are instead leading. You are letting them manage themselves. This will allow you to use your time and energy in a more productive, more rewarding way, you'll be able to do more for the organization, and you'll open up better career opportunities for yourself.

WITH YOUR PEERS

Your relationship with your peers is probably the most complex one among all your relationships at the workplace. First, your peers are not necessarily required to work with you. Second, it's always possible that some of them will perceive you as a potential competitor. Depending on how you relate to each other, they can be your friends, your partners, your competitors, or even formidable foes.

See Your Peers Their Way

You already know that everyone has his or her own self-perception, and it is typically not that accurate. This usually varies considerably from person to person. While some people's perceptions of themselves can be quite accurate, other people's can be mostly inaccurate.

However, regardless of how accurate or inaccurate it is, you must respect a person's self-perception and appear to concur if you want to connect with that person successfully. At the very least, don't make others feel that you perceive them as less than they think they are worth. When others see that you know them so well, not only will they appreciate it, but they'll also be more likely to regard you positively.

Relationship

For most of us, it's easy to do so when we do perceive others in the same way they perceive themselves. But what if we perceive them quite differently? Is it still possible to let them see that we perceive them as they perceive themselves?

The answer is yes. The way to do it correctly is not to do much about it. You don't have to say how good or how wonderful others are. Just accept them for who they are, make them feel comfortable, and show that you respect them. It's important that you don't overpraise them, as this might actually do more harm than good.

A subtle thing that many people appreciate is your asking for help. The reason is that it makes others feel good about their expertise and about themselves. However, it only works well when what you are asking isn't difficult for others to do, and you don't ask too much of it. Otherwise, you risk annoying others or being seen as an incompetent person.

For the same reason, when you offer help or favors to others, ask yourself why you are doing it. Is it because you think they need it, or because you want to feel good about yourself? If others don't really need what you are offering, they may not want your help, and they may become annoyed by your generosity or kindness.

Chapter 6

But don't let these words stop you helping others. If others truly need your help, or the help is beneficial to both of you, they'll certainly appreciate your help when you offer it. Just don't overdo it. Don't make others feel that they have to accept your help.

Likewise, be careful when offering others advice. Although it might seem the right thing to do, and others should be appreciative, it's actually not so simple. Those to whom you are offering suggestions may not want to be seen as lacking the ability to solve their own problems. As a result, they may not want to hear your advice.

Of course, while showing respect to your peers, it's equally important that you culture their respect for yourself. The key to building a productive relationship with your peers lies in your ability to manage the two opposite yet complementary aspects. You will definitely have a productive relationship with them if you do the two things successfully.

Seek Win-Win

Again, one thing that may complicate your relationship with your peers is that you may see each other as competitors in the workplace. To some extent, it's true.

Relationship 151

It's usually easier to manage your relationship with those peers whose job is different from yours. However, wisdom and tact are needed to successfully manage your relationships with those peers whose jobs are similar or identical to yours. In particular, it's always a tactful task to manage your relationship with your peers on the same team as you. Everyone wants the team to succeed as a whole. Everyone also wants to be the best individual player. In order to manage the situation effectively, it requires you to know how to do it up front.

It's important to note that competition is not necessarily a bad thing. It can make people work that much harder and bring out people's best. There is nothing wrong with competition and wanting to be the best player. Without competition, we might not do more, and we might achieve less.

It's just that it also requires cooperation with one another and allowing others to shine too. Otherwise, it can lead to a zero-sum game for the team. When the team loses, no one wins. Choosing both cooperation and competition is the best choice for everyone.

It's especially vital for top players in a team to put cooperation ahead of competition. If you

Chapter 6

are already a top player, your own success on the job largely depends on the success of the team task. If the team fails, you achieve nothing, and it's quite possible that the blame for failure will land on your shoulders. Therefore, use discretion in making sure that you put the team's interests ahead of everything else, for it ultimately will serve your own interests as well. Don't think as an individual member. Otherwise, the team may not deliver satisfactory results, and you may not advance your career as quickly as you would like.

On the other hand, be sure that you always perform your best. You always need to develop your influence on the job. I wish I could say that you just need to be a nice person and everything will automatically work out well for you. That's usually not the case.

Of course, you don't have to engage in battles with others to demonstrate that you are a competent player. You don't have to be an aggressive person to develop your influence. You can actually do it in a much better way.

Whenever you make general remarks about anything, be committed to what you say and speak assertively (but not aggressively). It's very important that you talk assertively not only in

Relationship

meetings, but in all places all the time. When you demonstrate dynamism successfully, others will sense your strength, and it will produce amazing effects in others' minds. As a result, people will tend to recognize and be receptive to your influence, and you will be able to work effectively with them.

The best thing about this approach is that you can effectively influence others, yet no one will feel offended. After all, you are only making general remarks that aren't aimed at a specific person. It's unlikely that someone will have a problem with that.

When you demonstrate that you are an influential player, it will also help draw others to you. Many people will want to be your friends and have good relationships with you. They will want to avoid conflict with you whenever possible.

In order to achieve the best results, be sure to begin the process as early as possible. It's best to perform to your best ability from the beginning. Don't wait until you have a particular title to start the process. Once you have developed your influence effectively, people will think that you qualify to have the title and treat you as if you have it already.

Chapter 6

It's also important to keep in mind that even if you do everything perfectly, occasionally you might still have a problem with others. If anyone challenges you for any reason, be committed to what you believe is right. Make your case both calmly and firmly. When you resolve the matter in a composed yet firm manner, it will help you convince everyone that you are a more qualified player.

Again, while making sure that you develop your influence and perform effectively in your job, also make sure that you are respectful to your peers and are happy to see them performing well. You won't be able to develop your influence successfully without this open mind. If you can do the two mutual things effectively at work, you'll have a win-win relationship with your peers.

Ultimately, when all is said and done, there are two things you need do well in order to have a productive relationship with others. One thing is to treat yourself well and culture respect for yourself. The other is to respect others and be fair to them at the same time.

In essence, this eventually comes down to the three essential qualities: competency, goodwill, and dynamism. If you can demonstrate the three

Relationship

qualities effectively, you will be perceived in a desirable way, you will have good experiences with other people, and you will enjoy great relationships with them.

7

THE ULTIMATE SECRETS

Don't Be Overly Concerned with Perception

The first secret is that when you perform, don't worry about how others will judge your performance. If you think too much about other people's opinions of you in the middle of your performance, that concern may distract your mind from your performance, and you may perform less well as a result.

Even if you aren't onstage, you still shouldn't be overly concerned with others' perception of you. That concern isn't always helpful, especially if you let it preoccupy your mind too much.

The Ultimate Secret

Therefore, while you should pay attention to how others perceive you, be sure to calibrate the amount of attention you pay to it. As you know, many things in life are paradoxical.

The amount of attention should be such that you are mindful enough of others' perception of you, yet it doesn't seem that you care too much about it. It's important to focus on your performance. When you perform successfully, a great by-product is that people will naturally perceive you in a delightful way.

It's for this same reason that you should be committed to your message in order to speak assertively and make your body language click well with your verbal message, as we discussed earlier.

SYNCHRONIZE YOUR HEART AND MIND

For many of us, this can be easier said than done. Although it's not a problem for some people to focus exclusively on their performances, it can be challenging for others. It has a lot to do with people's personalities.

However, regardless of what your personality is, the following will help you focus on your performance. If you incorporate these things into your performance, you are more likely to perform successfully.

First, it's important that you really care about what you are saying or doing. You already know the importance of commitment to your effectiveness. You can ask yourself to be committed, but the most effective way to do it is to make sure that you really care about what you are saying or doing. It should be something you truly believe in and feel strongly about.

When you have that much passion in what you believe in, and really mean it, it's unlikely that your commitment won't look genuine or natural. Your heart will be doing the job, and your body language will certainly be authentic. You won't just appear convincing. You will truly be convincing.

This will also make your communication truly engaging to others. Even if you can't convince others of what you are saying, it's unlikely that they will doubt your convictions. What's more, you won't have to try to be yourself. You will naturally be yourself—your most effective and best self.

In order to be so committed to what you are saying or doing, it helps to have a goal in mind.

The Ultimate Secret

When you know what you really want, not only will it help you find your direction in life, but it can automatically keep you committed to what you want to accomplish. A goal will unleash the incredible power within you.

But make sure that you don't have so many goals that they conflict with one another. Otherwise, you may not really know what you should be truly committed to. It's better to have one accomplishable goal than many that end up not only unheeded, but also wasting much of your time, talent, and energy.

We have already discussed the importance of preparation, but it is worth addressing a second time. It always helps to do your homework first. This is especially important if you are unfamiliar with what you need to perform. Your preparation will arm you with knowledge, skills, and whatever else you might need. It can also help you relieve any concerns that you might have about your performance. When you are well prepared, you will gain more confidence in yourself, and you will be able to perform most successfully.

If you keep doing your homework, it will also make your future performance much easier for you. By doing all the homework and perform-

160   *Chapter 7*

ing, your ability will grow, and you will naturally perform even better.

This also applies to managing your personality. Your personality is largely controlled by your primitive brain, and it tends to show consistency across various situations for a long period. The primitive brain is intuitive. It learns through experience or actually doing certainly things repeatedly. If there is anything about your personality that you want to improve, it helps to practice it repeatedly. Once you've done it enough times, you'll be able to apply it automatically in real situations.

For example, let's say you want to make sure that you will keep your cool in all situations. You can ask someone to throw an angry "punch" at you, and then practice your cool response. It really works when you practice more.

Although it sounds simple, this role-playing exercise is an effective way to train our primitive brains. You can improve virtually any skill by practicing it. Just don't do it merely once or twice and then forget about it. You may have to practice it a bit more in order to see results.

It's also important to be consistent with your performance. If you have just one role to play,

The Ultimate Secret

it's always easier than playing many different roles. When you are always the same person, it will definitely help ease your mind.

This will also make it easy for others to know you well. When you maintain a steady performance, others will be more likely to think that it is really you, and they'll be more likely to recognize and accept your performance.

LIGHTEN UP

The second secret is that while you should do your best, when you perform, don't overexert yourself, and don't overdo it. As mentioned earlier, many things in life are paradoxical. If you take yourself too seriously, care too much about what others think of you, or have to see a particular outcome in everything, that kind of thinking can eventually do more harm than good.

To avoid that from happening, it's important to realize that we are only human. None of us is perfect, and we will never be. So be reasonable in everything. Don't expect too much, and don't be a perfectionist.

What's more, life is more than just work. For example, it's also important that you don't stress

Chapter 7

yourself and everyone out. But if you are too intense about what you are doing, that kind of intensity may wear out everyone, not to mention that it doesn't necessarily produce the best results.

There is always a force associated with the way you present yourself. If you overexert yourself, the force can be more negative than positive, and it may alienate you from others. When you ease up, you'll be able to make others feel comfortable, they will be more likely to like you, and you will be able to work with them most effectively.

Indeed, when you ease up, you will actually perform better and enjoy your job a lot more. It'll enable you to control your emotions and keep your cool, you can therefore balance your goodwill and dynamism ideally, and you will have the sophistication to perform at the highest level.

Of course, be sure that you still make your best effort. It's just that you should also relax, lighten up, and be human. This will make your performance most productive, most enjoyable, and long lasting.

PART III

REVIEW AND ADJUSTMENT

8

MAKING CHANGES

IF YOU ARE UNSATISFIED

If you don't like other people's perception of you, it must be that somehow you haven't present yourself in a productive manner, or that you haven't used your talent effectively. It's vital to realize there is a problem in the way you present yourself or use your talent. This will help you come up with a solution, fix the problem, and turn the situation around.

The best way to do that is to make effective changes so that others can take a new look at you. If you still do the same thing over and over, others may not see your virtues as clearly as they should, and their perception of you may not change.

The reason is that others' old perception of you can make them see you and judge you in just one way. As we discussed earlier, perception is a single-minded force. People tend to see only those things consistent with their perceptions.

However, when you make notable changes, the new things you do will have a much better chance of catching people's attention, and they may thus look at you in a new way. In order to make others perceive you differently, change is the best opportunity.

We talked about "primacy effect" earlier in the book. It refers to the fact that people tend to weigh early information much more heavily than later information when judging others. In contrast to the primacy effect, there is also a phenomenon termed "recency effect." It refers to the fact that people may weigh later information much more heavily than early information.

Is there a conflict between the primacy effect and recency effect? The answer is no. The primacy effect always exists. However, in order to generate the recency effect, the new things must be somewhat impressive. If what occurs later is

Making Changes 167

not striking enough, it won't generate the recency effect.

That's why, in order to turn the situation around, making notable changes is necessary. It's best to create a shock to others' old perception of you. The more you make others look at you in amazement, the more effectively you can change their former beliefs about you.

In order for this to work, be sure that you know your strengths. It's important to do what you do best so that you can deliver excellent results in what you do.

It's also important to know what the critical issues are, what is valued more, or what others really pay attention to. These are the most rewarding tasks to tackle. Focus on one that you can do well, leverage your strengths, and do whatever is necessary to deliver the goods.

If you do so successfully, almost certainly others will look at you differently. If what you do is important to your boss, it's even better. If your boss is an emotional person, you may see the effect instantly. Out of all your colleagues, your boss's perception of you matters the most. If he or she begins to perceive you differently, you'll soon benefit.

Chapter 8

Then, be sure to maintain the momentum, and demonstrate that you are reliable and can be counted on. If, while others are still wondering whether they were wrong about you, you stop your efforts and drop your performance, others will know they were right about you after all. If you only perform now and then, it won't work too well.

If you are unsatisfied with others' perception of you, particularly your supervisor's, another way to address the situation is to change the environment or the people you work with. If you move to a different department, or a different organization altogether, the old perception and the associated force will automatically disappear, and you can start anew. Of course, don't just change the environment and see how it goes. In order to make it work well, it's vital to do everything right in your new environment.

IF YOU ARE ALREADY HAPPY

Hopefully, you've done very well and enjoy an excellent perception of yourself at work. If so, you'll benefit tremendously, for the favorable perception of you will be a powerful competitive edge.

Making Changes

Nevertheless, it's important to keep performing well in order to maintain others' favorable perception of you. If you want to continue advancing your career, you may even have to upgrade their perception of you, especially if you have advanced your career to midlevel positions.

The reason is that what has carried you to your current place may not continue carrying you to higher places. The expertise and skills that have made your performance successful so far may not be enough for you to perform even better in the future. If you keep performing the same ritual, you may plateau in your career. You may have to adjust what you've been doing in order to keep moving forward.

Of course, there is nothing wrong with not wanting to adjust what you have been doing. There is nothing wrong with doing what you do best. If it is important to you and continues making you happy, you should probably keep doing it.

However, if you want to achieve even more and keep advancing your career, you must adjust what you have been doing. You must let people see that you have more to offer and can do more.

For that purpose, while making sure that you are performing well in your current job function, be sure that you also think and talk more about strategic issues. The reason is that these are what top-level executives pay attention to and usually talk about. When you do that, you'll sound like a top-level executive, you'll be able to talk with them more, and you'll look qualified to fit top-level positions.

You may also need to improve your communication and people skills. The reason is simple. You need those skills to lead effectively and achieve good results through others. That is the way to leverage your knowledge and ability, and to achieve more.

It's important that you don't wait too long to take the initiative. Others' perception of you can form very fast. If they have already formed the perception that you probably can't do more, they may not expect you to do the job at the next level. Then you have to overcome the force of that perception, which can make the adjustment harder for you.

Essentially all midlevel managers today have the potential to become top-level executives tomorrow. Other than great results, the required credentials are excellent vision and communica-

Making Changes

tion skills. Whether you can keep moving up in your career will have a lot to do with how successfully you demonstrate these qualifications.

Therefore, be sure to demonstrate that you can see far and are a strategic thinker, and that you can lead successfully and achieve great results through others. Don't wait to act like a top-level executive after you become one. If you act like a top-level executive already, the perception will be that you should be one, and you will be more likely to become one.

EPILOGUE

Many years ago, I read somewhere that a person's experiences are his or her treasures. Somehow those words would appear in my mind again and again during the years, and I often wondered what I could do with my experiences. The writing of the book is probably the answer, and I'm so happy that I have done it.

Of course, no one can write a book that is tailor-made for everyone, and it is possible that only portions of the contents will fit your needs. If you have found resonance in the book, or if you have gotten something out of it, it'll mean that it was well worth the effort writing it. I hope it will make a difference in your career, and I wish you much success.

INDEX

Accomplishable goal 159
Accurate perception 32
Achievability 70, 72, 74
Acquire dynamism 128
Act decisively 142
Acting career 46
Actor 23, 46
Adequate results 75
Advance your career 152,
   169
Advantage 52
Advice 160
Advocating 111, 113
Agenda 62, 95
Ailes, Roger 101
Alert state 32
Ambiguity 95
Ambitious ideas 71
Amount of attention 157
Analogies 120

Analytical brain 37, 55,
   82
Angry 44, 124
Apparent confidence 51
Appearance 27, 91, 142
Arctic 54
Aristotle 39, 99, 124
Asking for help 149
Assertive 92, 93, 125, 142
Assumptions 27, 89
Attention 25, 99
Attitude 39, 57
Attorneys 103
Attractive packages 84
Audience 99
Average student 15
Avoid conflict 128, 153
Avoid unnecessary debate
   105

Index

Back burner 77
Balance your goodwill 40
Barrier 64
Beat uncertainty 66, 68
Beauty contest 52
Beauty index 56
Be consistent 34, 160
Be human 162
Being assertive 93
Benefit 112, 124, 125
Benton, Debra 57
Be open and direct 130
Be prepared 97
Berkeley, George 23
Best ability 153
Best choice 151
Best idea 73
Best makeup 56
Best player 151
Best results 153
Best shot 96
Better assessment 30
Between the lines 91
Be your best 28, 45, 47
Be yourself 93, 158
Bigger ideas 66
Body language 54, 55, 60,
     90, 91, 93, 157
Boxing match 52
Brand-new proposal 75
Build momentum 34
Build success 75
Bush, George W. 113
Business leaders 34

Business tasks 86
Button 79, 80

Candidate 23, 62
Career opportunities 147
Career prospects 61
CBS 46
Celebrities 46
CEO 35, 46, 57
Challenging task 71
Chances of success 96
Change the environment
     168
Character 23, 58, 62
Charisma 40
Charm 40
Children 31
Chinese philosophy 40
Chinese saying 37
City mayor 23
Civilization 23
Classroom 15
Clinton, Bill 107, 120
Coexist 40
Collaborate 96
Colleagues 75
Comfort zone 68
Commander in chief 36
Commendable person 127
Commitment 39, 58, 95,
     128, 158
Common characteristics
     57

Index

Communication 55, 60, 86, 88, 170

Competency 41, 78, 86, 136, 154

Competency component 39

Competent personality 41

Competition 24, 131, 151

Competitive edge 168

Competitors 148

Complementary aspects 150

Complementary forces 40

Complexity 72, 74

Concerns 111, 129, 139, 159

Confidence 51, 52, 59, 91

Confident appearance 56

Cons 97, 110, 111, 118

Consumers 84

Content of presentation 99

Control button 82

Conviction 91, 96, 110, 143

Cooperation 75, 151

Cooperative responses 57

Coordinating work 98

Correct answers 16, 30

Correct information 31, 33

Correct perceptions 33

Counterproductive manner 123

Court 103

Creativity 137

Credentials 170

Credibility 34, 69

Critical factor 34

Critical issues 167

Critical period 31, 34

Critical quality 58

Critical window 30

Criticism 66

Daring tactic 53

Debate 52, 101, 105

Debate know-how 109

Delegate tasks 146

Deliver results 69, 72

Demonstrate commitment 62

Demonstrate confidence 57, 142

Demonstrate creativity 137

Demonstrate dynamism 42, 58, 63, 130, 153

Desirable perception 29

Details 106

Develop your influence 152

Different idea 106

Different opinions 94

Difficult question 111

Dilemma 112, 129

Disagreement 108, 140,

143
Discouraging comments 67
Discussion 97, 108
Dominant role 29
Dynamism 39, 40, 51, 60, 104, 128, 130, 153, 154

Early impact 36
Early information 30, 166
Early period 30
Ease your mind 161
Effective boss 142, 143, 144
Effective communication 127
Effective image 72
Effective learning 78
Effectiveness in communication 56
Effective superior 142
Election 23
Emerson, Ralph Waldo 51
Emotional bond 82
Emotional brain 82
Emotional intelligence 38
Emotional needs 85
Emotional person 167
Emotional responses 56, 82, 84
Emotional results 81, 99

Emotions 56, 122, 162
Empathy 125
Energy 63
Engine 63
Ensure success 61
Entertainment industry 46
Enthusiasm 57, 147
Environment 168
Erroneous argument 114
Escort your confidence 59
Essential fundamentals 80
Essential ingredient 52
Essential knowledge 104
Exaggeration 115, 116
Exams 16, 24
Excel at work 134
Excel in debate 109
Excellent perception 168
Excellent results 167
Excelling 87
Exciting people 56
Exciting point 103
Execute the job 135
Executive Charisma 57
Exhibit confidence 58
Exhibit dynamism 40
Expand your capacity 47
Expand your strengths 76
Experience 27, 126
Expertise 39, 61, 104
Explanation 21
Expression of passion 63
External factors 44

Index

Extrapolate the
consequences 117
Exude confidence 51, 56
Eyeball movements 55
Eye contact 92

Facial expression 55, 90
Failure prevention 43
Favorable perception 168
FDR 102
Fear 66
Final perceptions 34
Final results 84
Fire 36
Firm manner 154
First impression 33, 37
Follow up 95
Force of perception 25,
26, 126
Former beliefs 167
Friends 148
Fundamental attribution
error 43, 122, 136
Future prospects 27

Gain leverage 34
GE 35
General remarks 152
Generate energy 63
Generosity 149
Gestures 55, 90, 93
Goal 158, 159

Goethe, Johann Wolfgang
26
Gold 27
Good ideas 135
Good intentions 64
Good listener 97, 124, 144
Good opportunities 65
Good results 107
Good start 37
Goodwill 39, 41, 104, 124,
128, 154
Grades 15
Grandest idea 73
Great by-product 157
Great communicator 101,
125
Great leaders 144
Great plans 71
Guarantee 97
Guideline 70, 108

Habit 78, 120
Halo effect 25
Harvest results 145
Healthy relationship 141
Heart 158
Heartbeat 98
Help 150
High-priority tasks 76, 77
Hire people 62
Holmes, Oliver 124
Homework 97, 159
Honor roll 15

Horns effect 25
Hostile questions 112
Hot seat 112, 119

Implementation 95
Important focuses 86
Important tasks 77
Incorrect assumptions 105
Incredible power 159
Individual member 152
Individual player 151
Inferences 89
Influence 62
Influential player 153
Inform your boss 138
Initial image 29
Initial impression 30
Initiative 68, 84, 170
Inner strength 61
Instinctive 37
Intelligence 110
Intensifier 42
Intentions 64
Interpersonal Perception 46
Interpersonal skills 86
Interviews 62
Introduction 102
Investment 136
Iraq 113
Irrelevant argument 118

Job function 170
Jones, Edward 29, 46
Judge 23
Junior professors 71
Jury 23

Keep your cool 124, 143, 160, 162
Kindness 149
Knowledge 21, 79
Know your message 97
Know your strengths 167

Language 90
Later information 30, 166
Law of perception 22, 24
Lawsuits 23
Lead 147, 170, 171
Learn everything 81
Learning sequence 79
Learning task 79, 81
Learn the ropes 43
Level of commitment 59
Leverage 167, 170
Life 162
Lighten up 162
Logical fallacies 114, 120
Losing focus 92
Low-priority tasks 77
Luntz, Frank 121

Index

Machiavelli, Niccol 27
Magic 42
Magic power 26
Maintain the momentum 168
Maintain your calm 123
Make assumptions 105, 143
Make changes 165
Make judgments 30
Making corrections 30
Managing your personality 160
Mankind 27
Mask 23
Maximize your effectiveness 130
Maximize your value 137
Meaningless question 111
Media 103
Meeting 97
Micromanage 146
Midlevel manager 62, 170
Midlevel positions 169
Mind 17, 82, 100
Misinterpret 31
Misjudge 122
Misunderstand 122, 130, 141
Mondale, Walter 101
Moonves, Leslie 46
Multiple-choice problems 29
Mutual things 154

Negative comments 67
Negative information 42
Negative remarks 107
Negative situations 44
Negativity effect 42, 98
New environment 168
New executives 71
New job 34
New knowledge 80
New leader 34, 37
New look 37, 165
New organization 30
New position 34, 35
Next level 83, 135
Niceness 128
Nice person 41, 152
Nobel Prize 72
Nonverbal expressions 55
Notable changes 166

Objections 95
Objective manner 82
Observations 32, 33
Obstacles 64
Offer help 149
Off guard 103
Old perception 166, 167
On Writing Well 85
Open mind 154
Opinions 16
Opportunities 65, 66
Outperform 15
Outsiders 35

Overcome Barriers 64
Overconfidence 58
Overpraise 149
Overreact 123

Partners 148
Passion 131, 146, 158
Peers 148, 151
People skills 170
Perceiver 24
Perception formation 32
Perception is reality 21
Perfect grades 15
Performance 45, 159
Performers 46
Persistent performance 98
Person 23
Persona 23
Personal factors 43, 70
Personal growth tasks 86
Personal impact 136
Personality 37, 157
Personality component 38
Personality traits 38
Phenomenon 30, 43, 166
Philosopher 23, 26, 27, 51
Physical standard 56
Pipa 53
Polar bear 54
Politeness 127
Positive comments 107
Positive effect 42, 43
Positive impact 97

Positive information 30, 42
Positive light 127
Positive responses 57
Positive thinking modes 106
Power of confidence 55
Power of perception 24
Power of performance 46
Practice 160
Praise 147
Preparation 97, 100, 159
Prerequisite 93
Presentation 45
Presidential communicator 101
Presidential episodes 102
Primacy effect 30, 166
Primal need 31, 33
Prime minister 36
Primitive brain 37, 55, 91, 160
Priorities 76
Proactive communicator 95
Problems 64, 138
Problem solving 98
Products 84
Project confidence 55
Project manager 140
Proposal 59, 60, 105
Pros 97, 110, 118
Psychological phenomenon 30

Index 183

Pure performance 45
Pushing your agenda 95

Qualified player 154
Questionable perception
    33, 69
Questionable process 45
Questions 111
Quick decisions 143
Quiz 29

Rapport 137
Reagan, Ronald 101
Real cause 136, 141
Real issue 112, 119
Reality 21, 22, 24, 27
Real player 61
Reason 106
Reason positively 82
Recency effect 166
Recognition 22
Rejection 66
Relationship 126, 132
Remote control 79, 80
Reports 141
Resistance 60, 67
Resources 135
Responsibility 133
Result-oriented learning
    79
Rewarding tasks 167
Rhetorical questions 113

Right information 29
Risk 73
Role-playing exercise 160
Roosevelt, Franklin D.
    68, 101

Safeguard your emotions
    123
Satisfactory results 77
School 15
Second opportunity 135
Secret 156
Self-fulfilling prophecy 26
Self-perception 148
Selling your message 110
Sensation 40
Shu Kingdom 36
Sima, Yi 53
Simple style 85
Simplicity 85
Single-minded 24
Situational factor 44, 70
Situational impact 136
Situational reasons 122
Slippery slope argument
    116
Small ideas 66
Society 22
Soft side 40
Soliciting support 107
Solid foundation 72
Solidification process 33
Solid rationale 121

Sophistication 162
Speak assertively 152
Speak convincingly 92
Speaker 99, 104
Speaking effectively 90
Speak out 90
Speak your mind 129, 131
Speech 100
Speed 35
Spirit 40, 52, 63
Spontaneous responses 37, 38
Sports coaches 103
Staff member 129
Stamina 76
Standard measurement 24
Stand your ground 95, 109, 113
Start the process 153
Statesperson 27, 36
Stay calm 123
Steady performance 161
Strangers 32
Strategic issues 170
Strategic self-presentation 46
Strategic thinker 171
Straw man argument 115
Strengthen your argument 120
Strengthen your dynamism 60
Strengths 75
Strong closing 103

Strong person 61
Subconscious process 27
Subjective judgment 24
Subordinates 142
Subtle clues 54
Successful image 51
Success strategies 34
Sufficient competency 41
Sufficient support 136
Super idea 73
Support 135, 136
Synchronization 98
Systematic learning 78

Tackle tasks 72
Take action 64
Take charge 43
Talk show 129
Team 151
Team member 140
Team task 152
Telling the truth 129
The Apprentice 140
The First 90 Days 34
Theory about presentation 99
The rules 17
Three essential qualities 38
Three Kingdoms Period of China 36, 52
Tonality 55, 90
Top-level executives 170

Index

Top players 151
Top student 15
Total efforts 151
Tough call 74
Trial and error 75
Tricky arguments 109
True nature 21, 27
Trust 137
Tully, Grace 101
Two-way process 124
Two essential ingredients 137
Type of person 44

Uncertain aspects 110
Uncertainties 67
Uneasiness 32
Unnecessary debate 105
Upbeat spirit 57
Up front 47
Uphill battle 34
Using knowledge 81

Valid argument 114
Valuable aspects 113
Verbal message 56, 91, 157
Verdict 23
Virtues 25
Virtuous cycle 34
Visibility 40
Vision 170
Voice volume 55
Voters 23

Watkins, Michael 34
Wei Kingdom 53
Welch, Jack 35
Wield influence 146
Win-Win 150, 154
Winfrey, Oprah 129
Wondrous quality 42
Words 90

Yin and yang 40
Your boss 73, 82, 131, 134
Your direction 159
Your effectiveness 133
Your influence 153
Your message 96
Your style 93
Your supervisor 133
Your true self 131
Your virtues 165
Your worth 133

Zero-sum game 151
Zhuge, Liang 36, 52
Zinsser, William 85